WHAT IS PERSON-CENTRED THERAPY?

A PERSONAL AND PRACTICAL GUIDE

BY

TONY MERRY AND BOB LUSTY

GW00535871

Published by Gale Centre Publications for

THE GALE CENTRE, WHITAKERS WAY, LOUGHTON, ESSEX IG10 1SQ.

Tel (0181) 508 9344. Fax (0181) 508 1240

Cover by Lizzie Spring   ISBN: 1 870258 40 1

Copyright: Gale Centre Publications 1993 (Reprinted 1995)

Published by Gale Centre Publications
Whitakers Way
Loughton, Essex
IG10 1SQ

© Gale Centre Publications, 1993

British Library Cataloguing in Publication Data

A CIP record for this book is available from the British Library

CONTENTS

PREFACE

Why a personal and practical guide?

The personal and practical guides aim to help you understand what a particular therapy is about and what it feels like to experience it and to be a therapist in it. The check lists, descriptions, exercises and case histories in the guides are designed to allow you to form an individual study programme or a study programme with a group of colleagues. This programme will not turn you into therapists nor will it enable you to work on a deep level on therapeutic problems and it is not designed with either of these aims in mind. What it will do is give you an experience of how the therapeutic method works by suggesting practical exercises you can do yourself. It will also give you an experience of what it feels like to be a therapist giving that sort of therapy, the sort of problems for which the therapy can be used to help and the likely outcome.

After this study programme you will at the very least know what the therapy is about and be able to talk coherently about it. You will also have a better idea of whether you would want to be a client in that form of therapy and whether you would want to develop an expertise in it. I also hope that experienced and practising therapists will be able to find elements in the therapies described which they will be able to use to supplement and develop their own skills.

It is generally a requirement of training as a therapist that the therapist undertake therapy. It often strikes me as odd that therapists writing about their work make only scant references to their own therapy.

Therapists seem to be particularly reticent in talking about their own therapy, yet at the same time maintain that there is no stigma attached to therapy.

Therapy is not a science, it is an art and research has shown that the individual qualities of the therapist are often more significant than the method used. It seems odd that so little writing about therapy includes the personal experiences of therapists and their difficulties and failures in therapy.

The current Green revolution and the growth of interest in alternative therapies means that we are starting to pull away from the deification of scientific objectivity. This poses a problem for psychotherapy which has for so long been trying to gain acceptance by the scientific community. In its attempt to gain respectability and distance from the parodies of the actor and cartoonist, psychotherapy has used a form of scientific research and writing which alienates therapy from its true roots which are in the arts and the social sciences and not the natural sciences.

If, as I believe, psychotherapy is a search for an answer to that most fundamental of questions "Who am I", it is as much a search for a personal morality as a cure for mental pain and psychological disease. Then there is every place for subjectivity in the process itself and in books there is a place for the personal history and the personality of the author.

Humanistic psychology tends to provide more space for human error and fallibility on the part of the therapist but even in that discipline there is not enough trust for people to really be open about themselves. In this series I have made no attempt to edit out the personal approach of the authors, far less my own personality. In fact, I have encouraged them to include their personal experiences. There are plenty of books on every method of therapy written from the so called objective viewpoint and this series is offered as a counterweight to them.

The personal and practical guides do not take part in the internecine nor the intranecine battles that proliferate in most therapies but aim to put its readers in an informed position where they can make up their own mind. I welcome feedback from readers and as the books are printed on short runs can often incorporate it in future editions.

A note on Gender: to avoid the awkwardness of phrases like him/or, he/she the male authors of the series are asked to use the words he, him, etc. while the female authors use the female pronouns.

Derek Gale.

CHAPTER ONE

INTRODUCING PERSON-CENTRED THERAPY

This book is about the Person-Centred Approach to counselling and psychotherapy. It is for counsellors and therapists, either practising or in training, and for people who use counselling skills as part of their work, but who don't want to be full time counsellors - nurses, teachers, social workers, personnel managers, and community workers, for example.

The Person-Centred Approach is a humanistic way of helping people that taps into the resources we all have for helping ourselves. Among counsellors and therapists, it is one of the best known of the "non-psychodynamic" approaches, but not always the best understood.

Although a book can never be a substitute for a proper training, this one involves you in experimenting, in a safe way, with the ideas and concepts it describes. It will be useful as part of a training course, but just as useful if you want to join with a group of friends or colleagues and become better at forming good, helpful relationships with the people you meet and work with.

You will find that most books about the Person-Centred Approach (PCA) are written in the USA, and, obviously, have an American readership in mind. An exception is *Person-Centred Counselling in Action*, by Brian Thorne and David Mearns. *What is Person-Centred Therapy?* is different in that it invites you to try out some of the skills and qualities of Person-Centred therapy for yourself, and it gives you ideas about how to go about doing it.

1

Many books on therapy and counselling are good at describing the theory, and often give case-studies and examples of how therapy works in real life. However, it is hard to find books about the PCA that help you develop the attitudes, values and qualities that good PCA therapists and counsellors need. *Exercises in Helping Skills* by Gerard Egan is for the "generic counsellor", and doesn't concentrate on the PCA as such. The same is true of *The Theory and Practice of Counselling Psychology* by Richard Nelson-Jones. The present book is an exception in that it concentrates more or less exclusively on Person-Centred therapy, but it isn't a "DIY" manual for therapists who have no other training or experience in therapy. In other words, we don't pretend that reading this book (or any book) will turn you into a therapist.

The Person-Centred Approach also has much to offer even if you don't work as a therapist, or use counselling skills in your work. The PCA is about relationships, communication, understanding and creativity, and most of us would benefit from having more skill and learning in these areas. We have set out to do two things. One is to introduce you to the theory, philosophy and practice of Person-Centred therapy as clearly and concisely as we can. The second is to suggest ways in which you can use this book to explore the theory, skills and attitudes we describe, so that they feel more alive. Although we concentrate mainly on Person-Centred theory and practice, we have included some brief discussions of more general aspects of therapy. This is so you can see how the Person-Centred Approach fits in with the picture of counselling and psychotherapy in Britain today.

The way to fully understand any form of therapy is to experience it for yourself. This lets you know what it's like from the inside. In this book we say what Person-Centred therapy means to us, we write about how we help to prepare people to become therapists, and we say something of our own experiences as clients and therapists, but obviously this isn't a substitute for a proper training, or for the experience of being a client.

About the authors

Our backgrounds are in Higher Education. We teach counselling and counselling psychology, see clients regularly, supervise individuals and groups of therapists and counsellors, and we are accredited counsellors with the British Association for Counselling (BAC).

Our philosophy of therapy is Humanistic, which means we see people as capable of growth and change throughout their lives, and that personal freedom and social responsibility are two sides of the same coin. We see most mental illness and psychological disturbance as part of the struggle to become more human in an increasingly distressing and confusing world. And we see psychotherapy as one way to help us make sense out of life and live at peace with ourselves and each other.

About Carl Rogers

Person-Centred therapy was developed by Carl Rogers, an American psychologist and psychotherapist, who died in 1987. He was one of the founders of Humanistic Psychology, and his influence and ideas have now spread around the world.

Carl Rogers is such an important figure in the development of psychotherapy, that it will help to know a little more about him before you read the rest of this book because his life and work were so tied together. A new biography of Carl Rogers by Brian Thorne has recently been published (see booklist), so we need give only a few details here.

Born in 1902 in Oak Park, near Chicago, Rogers first started working as a psychologist in New York, with the Society for the Prevention of Cruelty to Children. After a while, he became disenchanted with what he saw as mainstream psychology, with its emphasis on testing and treatment, and began to develop his own theories and ways of working with clients. He disliked the way psychology, at that time, seemed to treat people as objects for study rather than as people needing understanding and compassion.

What was at first known as "non-directive therapy" became more widely known with the publication of Rogers' book, *Counselling and Psychotherapy - Newer Concepts in Practice*. By the early 1950's, non-directive therapy became known as "client-centred therapy", particularly after the publication of *Client-Centred Therapy : Its Current Practice, Implications and Theory*.

Later, the term "Person-Centred Approach" was adopted when it was shown that the theory and philosophy of therapy could be adapted and transferred to other settings where people's growth and development were of central importance - like in education, for example. Rogers' best known book is *On Becoming a Person*, and it is probably through this book or his last one, *A Way of Being*, that most people discover Carl Rogers. In the 1940's and 1950's Rogers began to make sound recordings of therapy interviews (not easy in those days), and tried to identify the factors that seemed to be helpful and unhelpful in helping clients change. From these observations, he developed a theory of therapy and personal change that could be tested through further research and clinical experience.

Rogers devoted the last few years of his life mainly to writing and to peace work. He also ran workshops, gave demonstrations, and contributed to seminars in countries all round the world, including Poland, Hungary, England, South Africa, Ireland, South America and the then Soviet Union.

Therapy and the Person-Centred Approach

Person-Centred therapy is also known as "Client-Centred" therapy, and more generally as the "Person-Centred Approach", and this can lead to some confusion. We take the term "Person-Centred Approach" (PCA) to refer to a set of attitudes, values and a philosophy that can be applied to any setting where people's personal growth and development is of concern. For example, there is a Person-Centred Approach to education, which applies Person-Centred philosophy to the classroom and lecture room, a Person-Centred Approach to management, to cross-cultural communication, conflict exploration, and so on.

Occasionally we read references to "Person-Centred Hypnotherapy", or "Person-Centred Gestalt", for example, and we think this is very misleading. Hypnotherapy and Gestalt proceed from quite different assumptions about how personal change and development takes place, and have quite different views about the role of the therapist. It does seem strange to us when people put the term "Person-Centred" in front of other approaches when there is such a mismatch of basic philosophy and processes.

In this book we present Person-Centred therapy in its traditional form, which means we believe Person-Centred therapy to be, of itself, an effective means of promoting personal change, and does not benefit from being mixed up with other approaches.

Is it psychotherapy or counselling?

There are many points of view about the differences between psychotherapy and counselling. In this book, we use the terms "psychotherapy", or just "therapy", but we could just as easily have used the term "Person-Centred counselling". We think the distinction between counselling and psychotherapy, if there is one, is very difficult to make with any real precision.

At one time, counselling was thought of as short term, and psychotherapy as long term, but now there is increasing interest in brief psychotherapy, and counsellors sometimes work with clients for fifty or sixty sessions or more, so where does that leave us?

Another distinction is that counselling is believed to be concerned with identifiable problems, and psychotherapy with more deep seated psychological disturbance. But more and more counsellors are finding that they cannot confine themselves to working only with identifiable problems, which may represent only the tip of an emotional ice-berg.

Finally, it is thought that counsellors and psychotherapists have different training requirements. Psychotherapists have long periods of intensive training, which usually includes their own therapy or analysis. Counsellors, on the other hand, have much shorter training, and are not necessarily required to undergo their own therapy.

There is some truth in this, but the picture has changed a lot in recent years. Most training institutes in Person-Centred therapy of which we know, offer training periods of up to three years of part-time study (please see the Resources section for details). If they don't actually require their students to be in personal therapy as part of the training process, they do advise them to enter personal therapy before starting to see clients themselves.

The social context of therapy

Therapists and counsellors do not work in isolation from the rest of the society and culture in which they live. Our society is rich in cultural differences, and is also one in which some people enjoy more power and privilege than others. Therapy can be criticised for being available more to the relatively well and economically advantaged than to the very disturbed, poor or otherwise disadvantaged.

Getting a therapist often involves paying fees - there is some counselling and psychotherapy available from the National Health Service, but it is limited - so this fact alone means that some people who need it cannot afford to pay for it. This is not an argument against therapy, but it is a reminder to would-be therapists that they may find it difficult to work with some clients whose need may be great, but whose capacity to pay is limited or non-existent.

The social context also includes groups who have particular needs, different from those of the majority. Such groups include members of cultural or ethnic groups whose attitudes to therapy, and what they need from it, may be very different from those of the majority. It is also likely that many such groups (if not all) will have experienced prejudice or some form of discrimination, and may therefore be justifiably suspicious of what therapy has to offer if it remains a largely white, middle-class activity.

Although therapy certainly isn't politics, it does have a political dimension which therapists need to acknowledge and, more importantly, do something about. At the very least, therapists should be aware of the social and cultural values they hold, and be prepared to confront the racism, sexism and other "isms" they have unwittingly absorbed, in an effort to be free of unhelpful attitudes towards people who have very different experiences and expectations.

Therapists will be more effective if they are aware of the social backgrounds and contexts of their clients, and knowlegeable enough to see how different people bring different experiences and expectations with them into therapy sessions. Being understanding of individuals includes being sensitive to the cultural norms and values that influence different people to see things in very different ways.

The practice of psychotherapy and counselling is becoming much more of a distinct profession these days, with increasingly rigorous rules and codes of conduct. In Britain, the British Association for Counselling (BAC) has developed an accreditation procedure through which people may apply for professional recognition of their training, experience and competence. To be accredited, people have to be able to show they have had appropriate training, and experience of working with clients under supervision. They also must agree to abide by the BAC Code of Ethics. At present, accreditation is voluntary, and not linked to any form of registration.

The BAC also has a recognition procedure for courses in counselling and psychotherapy. To be recognised, a course has to be substantial in terms of time and content, and must meet a number of quite strict criteria. When you have successfully completed a BAC recognised course, it is assumed that the training requirement for individual accreditation has been met, but you would still have to complete 450 hours of supervised practice over three years before accreditation could be given.

There is now a separate body, the U. K. Council for Psychotherapy (formerly UKSCP), whose aim is to establish professional standards for training and qualifications in psychotherapy. Membership of this conference includes representatives from the majority of training organisations in psychotherapy, and representatives of allied professions like the Royal College of Psychiatry, the British Psychological Society, and the British Association of Social Workers.

Ethical issues in psychotherapy

People who enter psychotherapy can be in a vulnerable and anxious state. They may recently have had experiences which have left them with lowered self-esteem, or even feeling worthless and unloved. In such states, people are much more open to being exploited than when they are more at peace with themselves, and it's easier for them to fall prey to unscrupulous and unethical practices.

These range from keeping clients dependent for longer than necessary in order to keep collecting fees, through to sexual exploitation. A therapist can be quite a powerful figure in the lives of lonely or unconfident people, and people can develop quite strong feelings towards someone who appears to be wise and "together", and is giving them time, care and attention.

If a counsellor or therapist is a member of a professional body, he or she will be bound by a code of professional ethics. The BAC, for example, has a code of ethics which is quite clear on matters of unprofessional conduct. This code states, for instance, that it is always unethical for counsellors to engage in sexual activity with clients.

Another ethical issue concerns supervision. Again, the BAC is quite clear about this, and insists that all counsellors accredited by them are in regular contact with an experienced supervisor. This is to help ensure that a counsellor's practice remains ethical and professional, and to provide somewhere where the counsellor can go to discuss problems or misgivings.

About the exercises and checklists in this book

We think you will find this book useful as part of a training programme, or as a means of helping you discover ways in which you can become more effective in your own professional and personal relationships. The exercises and checklists

8

are designed to help you experience what we are describing, rather than just reading about them.

The best way to approach them is to get together with a small group and work your way through them. There should always be time at the end of each exercise for general discussion and sharing of the things you have learned. Most of them can also be done on your own as a way to check what you are reading and learning about psychotherapy.

Before you go on to the next chapter, explore what you know and think you know about Person-Centred therapy at the moment by working through the checklist that follows. It may be that you have heard some things about Person-Centred therapy, some of which may be accurate and some not. Every form of psychotherapy gives rise to myths, legends and misunderstandings about itself. When you have finished the book and tried some of the exercises, come back to this checklist and see if your ideas about Person-Centred therapy have changed.

CHECKLIST 1 - TRUE OR FALSE?

1. Person-Centred therapists think that people are basically good.

    AGREE/DON'T KNOW/DISAGREE

2. Person-Centred therapy is OK for relatively well people, but no good for very disturbed people.

    AGREE/DON'T KNOW/DISAGREE

3. Person-Centred therapy is where you repeat what the client has said.

    AGREE/DON'T KNOW/DISAGREE

4. Person-Centred therapists do whatever they feel like doing.

    AGREE/DON'T KNOW/DISAGREE

5. Person-Centred therapy doesn't have a theory of personality.

    AGREE/DON'T KNOW/DISAGREE

6. Person-Centred therapy can't cope with evil or destructive people.

    AGREE/DON'T KNOW/DISAGREE

7. Person-Centred therapy is good for establishing rapport with clients, but then you need a lot of technique to treat them.

   AGREE/DON'T KNOW/DISAGREE

8. Person-Centred therapy can't help people with problems like fear of confined spaces, or obsessions etc.

   AGREE/DON'T KNOW/DISAGREE

9. Person-Centred therapy is too slow, and doesn't go "deep enough" really to help people much.

   AGREE/DON'T KNOW/DISAGREE

10. Person-Centred therapy is best used with a mixture of other techniques and methods.

   AGREE/DON'T KNOW/DISAGREE

CHAPTER TWO

PERSON-CENTRED THERAPY IN PRACTICE

In this chapter, we use a practical example of a therapy interview as a way to introduce the theory. Then we look again at the interview and see what it is that makes it Person-Centred, and examine what the therapist is trying to do, and how he does it.

A Person-Centred therapy interview

(The scene is the therapist's office. The client, Jack, has never been to a therapist before, so he is understandably a little nervous.)

Therapist: (In a welcoming and warm tone of voice) *Hello, Jack. Do make yourself comfortable. We've got almost an hour, would you like to tell me something about why you have come here today?*

Client: *Well, there are so many things. I don't know if you can help with them...It just seems that everything gets on top of me so easily these days, much more than they used to. I suppose I have been having a bad time lately. I don't seem to get on with my teenage daughter like I used to.... I feel very unhappy at work, maybe I've been there too long. My wife and I seem to be at each other's throats... I don't know.. coming to a therapist seems like a last resort, but I can't keep going like this much longer.*

Therapist: *Ok, there's a lot going on for you at the moment; it seems like it's been building up lately and it's getting harder to cope with...*

Client: *Yes, too many things, and all at once. Maybe I'm getting older....it feels like I'm losing my way or something. Life doesn't have the same happiness I used to feel. It makes me feel I'm just whingeing when I try and talk about it to anyone. Really there's nothing definite I can put my finger on, but sometimes I just want to chuck it all in..... but really I'm just so unhappy....*

Therapist: (Manner is tentative, exploratory) *So it's a feeling of just drifting, is it? Life seems to have lost its purpose or something like that? Not one thing, no crisis or anything, but you just feel so much sadness, and maybe a bit alone with it?*

Client: *I do feel a bit on my own. In fact I feel alone a lot of the time. Because there isn't anything specific, I can't really talk much about it. My wife says I'm moody and closed off... but how do you talk about something and nothing? It all seems a bit futile.*

Therapist: (Slightly rewords the client's question) *How can you open up when you don't really know what it is yourself..? But you do feel the loneliness, and* (with warmth) *I do hear the sadness in your voice.*

Client: *I just feel like I'm complaining when I have no real right to. I've got everything I need... why do I feel so, so unhappy?*

Therapist: (Reflects, is tentative) *It feels so unreasonable to complain, make a fuss, when there doesn't seem to be a real reason?*

Client: *Yes, I've always believed you should be happy with what you've got, there are so many worse off....I mean I'm not starving or in the middle of a war or anything. It's so hard to talk about this....it would almost be better if I did have some big issue that I could point to and say: "This is what's making you unhappy", but there isn't anything.... it all feels a bit phoney, making a mountain out of a molehill.*

Therapist: *It doesn't seem right just to say: "Look, I'm unhappy and I don't know why."*

Client: *No, it doesn't. I usually just keep these things to myself. Most people would never suspect I feel this way. I know my wife knows I'm unhappy. I think she's a* *bit scared of it, as if it's something to do with her. I want to tell her it isn't, but if we do start to talk about it we end up rowing, or I deny there's anything wrong.*

Therapist: (Summarises) *It's like you're used to sitting on your feelings, not letting them out, as if it's not quite right to do that. And if you do start to talk a bit, it all goes wrong, something like that ?*

Client: Yes, *and that makes it worse....It just seems to make things worse. Like I want to tell her it's not her, but I think sometimes I do end up blaming her, or at least she feels like I am. I mean, I know that it's me, something in me that isn't happy being who I am, doing what I do* (sighs, shakes head slowly)... *but how do you change that when you don't really know what it is?*

(Pause)

Client: *When I think about that, about what I just said, it does feel like there's another person in me, or perhaps it's another bit of me,* (sighs)... *who has kept quiet for a long time, and not really been happy with what's going on. I mean, the main bit of me is successful and all that, but .... I need to think about this more...*

(Quite a long pause, looks at therapist, shakes head and shrugs.)

Therapist: (Warm tone, quiet voice, hesitant) *As if there's part of you that has been ignored for a long time, not taken into account or something?*

Client: (A little more animated) *It seems weird, but it does feel a bit like that. Like someone got left behind in the rush to get on with things. But now it's beginning to feel like that part is saying: "What about me?" That scares me a bit, that thought....*

This dialogue is a fairly accurate reconstruction of a real interview that went quite well, and is quite typical of the kind of thing that happens in the early stages of Person-Centred therapy. The problem with the written word is that it doesn't capture the warm tone of the therapist's voice, or the slightly despairing and weary voice of the client, though the stage directions in brackets help a little. We can take a closer look at it, and try and see what makes this typically Person-Centred and different from other kinds of therapy.

13

Clients, not patients

The first thing to notice is that Jack is referred to as a client and not as a patient. At first, this might seem trivial, but really it is quite significant. Carl Rogers took the view that the people who came to him for help were not sick, like patients in hospital. He believed that we are all responsible people, potentially able to take charge of our own lives, with our own resources for change and growth.

Calling Jack a "client" implies that his unhappiness is a temporary state, *and that he has an active part to play in the process of feeling better about himself.* The Person-Centred therapist has the skills and qualities to be a companion to Jack as he explores his own world in his own way, and does not see clients as dependent and powerless.

This means that one of the first concerns of the Person-Centred therapist is to act consistently with the belief that the power to change resides in clients themselves, and not within therapists or their techniques. This central idea is so important in Person-Centred therapy, that it needs to be attended to right from the start of the therapeutic relationship. The ways in which therapists greet their clients, discuss fees with them, set out their therapy rooms and so on, all contribute to establishing a situation in which clients are respected, valued and trusted to make decisions for themselves.

Listening, Understanding, Communicating

The next thing to notice from reading the extract, is that the therapist concentrates on trying to *understand* his client - what he is saying, how he is feeling. He attends to all of the client's communication; not just the words, but also the tone of voice and other non-verbal clues.

The therapist is continually checking the extent to which he has accurately understood his client. But understanding, of itself, is of no value unless Jack knows he is being understood, so the therapist is also trying to communicate his understanding as clearly and sensitively as he can.The kind of understanding that tries to see what life is like for another person, without judging it or evaluating it - is known as *empathy*. A good example of empathy occurs when our therapist says: "*So it's a feeling of just drifting, is it? Life seems to have lost its purpose, or something like that? Not one thing, no crisis or anything, but you just feel so much sadness, and maybe a bit alone with it?*"

Here, the therapist is quite tentative in his communication. He isn't trying to tell Jack what he is feeling, but is exploring how far he has accurately understood what Jack is trying to express.

The next thing is that the therapist is quite economical in his responses. He doesn't make any big speeches, or drift off into speculations. He tries to summarise what Jack is saying and to reflect both the content and the emotional meaning of his words.

Finally, the therapist goes just a little further than the client's spoken words: "*....and maybe a bit alone with it*"*?* The therapist has sensed something that Jack didn't quite say. From Jack's tone of voice or other non-verbal clues, he noticed a feeling of aloneness, and he tried to reflect that sensing back to Jack, again in a tentative, exploratory way. We can see from Jack's next statement that the therapist was right in his sensing.

Although we use the word "reflect" here, it does not imply a passive activity, and definitely not one that involves simply repeating clients' words back to them. Reflection of feelings is one of the processes that help us to check out our listening, and keep us on the right track. Carl Rogers preferred terms like "testing understanding", and this implies a much more active process.

Deep empathic understanding is all too rare in most people's daily lives, and is one of the qualities that makes the therapeutic relationship different from our usual relationships. Being deeply understood helps dissolve feelings of isolation and gives us the courage to risk expressing more of our thoughts and feelings. Although empathy is particularly highly valued in Person-Centred therapy, it is a core quality of almost all therapeutic systems. Without it, it is highly unlikely that any therapy will be successful.

In 1986, Carl Rogers underlined, in an article in the *Person-Centred Review*, the importance of empathy as he saw it:

"To my mind, empathy is in itself a healing agent. It is one of the most potent aspects of therapy, because it releases, it confirms, it brings even the most frightened client into the human race. If a person is understood, he or she belongs." (*Person-Centred Review*, 2, 125 - 140)

Empathy is usefully thought of as a process and a quality rather than simply as a skill. It is a process because it develops as time goes by; it arises out of the relationship between client and therapist, but it isn't left to chance. It is more likely to develop if therapists attend to and nurture their ability to see the world in the ways their clients see it. This is sometimes known as *entering into the frame of reference of another person*.

In our example, even though it is very early in the relationship, there is a sense that the two people are *mutually* engaged in exploring meanings and working towards understanding. In successful therapeutic relationships, mutuality can develop into an intimate and close sharing of thoughts, emotions and experiences.

Warmth, Respect and Positive Regard

Other characteristics of the above extract are the *warmth* and *respect* shown to the client. The therapist is relating to Jack as a person struggling to come to terms with new and vaguely frightening feelings. Carl Rogers called this therapist attitude *unconditional positive regard*. It means that the therapist is listening attentively and caring for his client. He *prizes* Jack as a unique, worthwhile and valued human being. A good example of this comes when the therapist says: "....*But you do feel the loneliness, and I do hear the sadness in your voice.*"

Of course, warmth can't be turned on and off like a tap. We use the word "warmth" here to indicate a welcoming, open approach by the therapist. Expressing warmth that you do not really feel would be seen through straight away by most people. Warmth, in the sense of affection or liking is something that either develops naturally, or does not happen at all. The expression "to warm to somebody" indicates that a process is under way.

We don't use the word "warmth" to mean the same thing as affection, although as therapists we often develop feelings of liking and affection for our clients. In this context, the opposite of warmth would be "distance" or being "over-objective" or "aloof".

Excessive warmth, or being over-friendly, especially early on in therapy, might make it hard for clients to express angry, hostile or destructive feelings. Being warm doesn't mean being protective, overly sympathetic or just plain nice. These things may make it very difficult, if not impossible, for clients to express anger, or disappointment or other strong feelings towards their therapists.

Unconditional positive regard doesn't mean that therapists have to approve of everything their clients do, especially as people often do very hurtful and destructive things to themselves and others. It means that the therapist understands and accepts people, as non-judgementally as possible, as imperfect and trying to rid themselves of destructive behaviour. Unconditional positive regard is aimed at the basic humanness present in us all, even though that humanness may have become very damaged.

Look also at the *rapport* the therapist is establishing with Jack. The two people present seem to be meshing quite smoothly. If you were able to see and hear this interaction, you would probably notice that the therapist's voice is calm and unhurried, and that this is more than just a conversation. There is a sense of purpose about it, one in which client and therapist are engaged in a process in which layers of meaning, experience and feeling are gradually being uncovered and talked about. This is often referred to as the *therapeutic alliance*, and it indicates that therapist and client are working closely together to explore the client's world.

Congruence, being "real", being yourself

There is another, very important, characteristic of this extract that is difficult to notice from the written word. It is sometimes termed *therapist congruence*.

Congruence, or authenticity, or realness, means that the therapist is trying to be who he is, meeting his client, Jack, face to face, respecting him as a person in his own right, and entering into a relationship with him as an equal. He isn't trying to be a magician, or an expert technician, or anything other than who he is.

In the context of therapy, congruence includes therapists being aware of the feelings that arise in them during the relationships they develop with their clients. Sometimes it is appropriate for therapists to share these feelings with their clients, particularly, but not only, when such feelings begin to interfere with the ability to listen attentively.

This is most likely to happen after therapy has been going on for a few sessions, when therapist and client have learned something about each other, and the therapist is beginning to get more of a picture of the client's experience and concerns. For example, a therapist may notice that whenever a particular client talks about the death of his mother, he tends to do so in a very matter-of-fact and seemingly unemotional way. Each time this happens, the therapist feels disturbed; this isn't the way this client usually talks about things. It is as if this client becomes some other person at these times, and the therapist feels he loses contact with him, finding it more and more difficult to understand how the client really feels about the loss of his mother.

This persistent, disturbed feeling makes it difficult for the therapist to listen properly, and he begins to lose touch even more with his client. The therapist decides to express this feeling and says: *"Whenever you talk about your mother's death, I feel as if I can't get near you. I feel like I'm being held at arm's length, as if you're saying: "Don't get too close to me with this." It feels uncomfortable to me, and I'm torn between wanting to help you explore your feelings, and respecting your need not to let me get too close to them."*

In this case, openly expressing this feeling to the client enabled the client to become more aware of how he needed to control his feelings about the death of his mother, almost to the extent of denying he was affected at all.

The disclosure of feelings should be approached with care and sensitivity. Sometimes, especially when difficult feelings like anger, for example, or fear or boredom, are involved, it is better for therapists to talk their feelings through with a supervisor or experienced colleague first.

In other words, congruence does not mean disclosing feelings in an undisciplined, or haphazard way. Sharing feelings with clients appropriately is one thing, taking over the therapy session and talking about yourself is something else.

In the psychodynamic approach, feelings that develop within the therapist that become directed towards clients are thought to be examples of *counter-transference*. In the above example, this might indicate that the therapist is experiencing his own mixed feelings concerning loss and bereavement, and unconsciously projecting them inappropriately onto his client. In Person-Centred therapy, feelings like these can become a useful part of the process, provided therapists are aware of them and are willing to explore them to see if they have any meaning for their clients.

The therapist as a person

This brings us to another very important characteristic of Person-Centred therapy. In many of the helping professions people are taught that getting too involved with clients is something to avoid. They are advised to retain a professional distance, to remain objective, and outside of the client's world.

On the face of it, this is good advice. To over-identify with clients in distress and to worry about their welfare excessively, might lead us to become so bound up in their worlds, that we find it increasingly difficult to return to our own. On the other hand, taking an objective, distant and uninvolved stance will have the effect that people see us as having only a professional interest in them, that we are not really concerned about them as individuals with unique life stories.

Person-Centred therapists try to engage with their clients in ways that go beyond simply taking a professional interest. They are prepared to be moved by their clients, to respond to them as one person to another, and to show genuine concern and care. Person-Centred therapy sees it as most important that therapists are aware of themselves in their relationships with clients, aware of all their thoughts, feelings and emotions.

Trust

Therapists who are able, empathically, to understand their clients, and who are non-judgmental and congruent, are likely to be regarded as genuinely trustworthy. Trust is an important element in all relationships - its presence enables us to be more open and less defensive with each other.

In therapy, trust is something that is earned as clients realise that their therapists are not concerned with manipulating them and that acceptance is not conditional on behaving in ways that will win approval. The openness of therapists to themselves as people and their willingness to share themselves with their clients, is part of the process of earning trust.

One understandable concern that clients have is: *"How far can I trust my therapist to accept parts of me that I can scarcely accept myself?"* If clients can begin to see us as genuinely concerned for them, that our unconditional positive regard is not just something we put on or use as a technique, then they can begin to see us as reliable and safe.

The client is in charge

Before we leave this extract, notice that at no time does the therapist attempt to direct the course of the dialogue. He does not ask any direct or leading questions in an attempt to get the client to talk about particular things. This is very characteristic of the Person-Centred Approach. The therapist does not offer any advice, or attempt to interpret the client's statements, and there is no search for a *diagnosis* of the client or his condition. Again, this is very typical of Person-Centred therapy which is very sceptical of the value of labels of any sort.

The core conditions of Person-Centred therapy

Apart from this attitude, that it is the client who is in charge of the therapeutic process, there are three main characteristics of Person-Centred therapy, which have become known as *the core conditions*, illustrated in our extract:

Empathy - the therapist tried to understand Jack, to see what life was like for him, to enter into his world as much as possible, and to communicate his understanding to him.

Unconditional positive regard - he did not judge, evaluate or interpret Jack's feelings or thoughts. He had a respectful attitude, and prized Jack's uniqueness and individuality.

Congruence - the therapist did not try to hide behind a facade, or pretend to be more of an expert on Jack than Jack himself. He tried to engage with Jack as an equal, and saw the process of therapy as a shared one.

Although it is useful to identify each of these conditions, and describe them separately, it should be remembered that it is the *combination* of these three things, and the fact that therapists are able to offer them consistently, that makes for an effective therapeutic relationship.

The therapeutic relationship...

These three characteristics can readily be thought of as attitudes displayed by the therapist; they do not describe techniques, and this is the most obvious difference between Person-Centred therapy and many other forms of therapy. In other words, Person-Centred therapy is built on the relationship between client and therapist, more than on techniques that can be learned. (This is not to say that there are no *skills* involved in Person-Centred therapy. We shall be looking more closely at this later.)

....Not just "technique"

It is partly because of this lack of emphasis on technique that Person-Centred therapy has been misunderstood in the past. Carl Rogers sometimes despaired at the way Person-Centred therapy was misrepresented (say what the client last said, say "Hm", ask open questions etc). While these things, and others, may be useful, they are not the essence of Person-Centred therapy. Rogers, as we've said before, even had difficulty with the term "reflection of feelings". For him, this was too passive. What he was doing was checking how well he had understood his clients' words and feelings. He was not passively "reflecting" in the way that a mirror reflects, but actively striving to understand his clients' ways of being ever more deeply.

Before going further, we suggest you look through the next checklist, which reviews the main points we have covered so far.

CHECKLIST 2 : PERSON-CENTRED PRACTICE

The Person-Centred therapist...

1. Aims to understand the client from the client's point of view.

2. Is exploratory and tentative, not dogmatic or diagnostic.

3. Is economical in using language.

4. Uses reflection to check understanding.

5. Is warm and inviting, but not overbearing or sentimental.

6. Establishes rapport and a working alliance.

7. Aims to be authentic, open and real.

8. Is engaged with clients, but not overwhelmed by them.

9. Earns the trust of clients through being open and non-judgemental.

10. Builds a relationship based on a "way of being", not on techniques or methods.

11. Does not direct or decide the content of therapy.

12. Encourages a mutual, co-operative process.

CHAPTER THREE

DEVELOPING PERSON-CENTRED SKILLS AND QUALITIES

The skills and qualities of the therapist...

All therapists (of whatever school of thought) need to be skilled at listening and communicating if they are to be effective in building and maintaining therapeutic relationships. They need to be able to communicate their empathic understanding, their personal congruence and their willingness to accept and respect their clients with as little judgement as possible. This is best summed up by the phrase *quality of presence,* meaning that it is the underlying attitudes and values of the therapist that help clients feel safe enough to explore difficult, or painful experiences. Therapists who stick rigidly to a set of rules, or who try to use whatever technique comes to mind, are in danger of making the process mechanical and contrived.

... and the role of the client

All of Rogers' research into what constituted effective therapy concentrated on the skills, qualities and attitudes of the therapist. Except indirectly, he did not concern himself with the part played by clients, other than to say that clients need to perceive and experience the core conditions in order to make use of them.

However, we do know some things about the ways in which clients affect the process of therapy and its outcomes. For example, clients who seem to benefit most from therapy are those who have a belief in the effectiveness of the therapeutic process, and a belief in their own capacity to change in positive ways.

Other factors include clients' motivation for change, the extent to which they are already able to form close relationships with others, and their expectations of what they might gain from therapy. Of course, these things are not confined to Person-Centred therapy, they are quite general factors affecting the outcome of all forms of therapy. In other words, therapy consists of a dialogue, and both therapist and client have a part to play in its success or failure.

In this book we are more concerned with ways in which we can become more effective in our efforts to help our clients whoever they are, than in determining who among them is most likely to benefit. This is an important issue, though, as it has a bearing on whether we accept someone for therapy, or refer them to other forms of help.

In the next chapter, we take a closer look at the theory and philosophy that underpins Person-Centred therapy. But first we can create a checklist of skills and qualities that typify good Person-Centred therapy. One way of thinking about skills is that they are ways to put attitudes and values into practice through behaviour. It is possible to become more skilled in listening and communicating so that what we mean is what we say, and how we are with our clients is how we like to be with them.

What follows concentrates on the skills and qualities that contribute to all good relationships, not only those between clients and their therapists. Though they are appropriate not only in therapy, they are probably more evident in the therapeutic hour because the therapist tries to communicate them and "be" them in a concentrated and disciplined way.

CHECKLIST 3 - THE SKILLS OF THE THERAPIST

Empathic Listening

In everyday life we tend to listen only partially; sometimes we may be rehearsing a response, or trying to construct an argument or in other ways paying only limited attention to what we are hearing.

In therapy, a different, more active and focussed listening is required. Empathic listening involves a process of sensing the meanings and half-hidden emotions which accompany whatever it is our clients are expressing. It involves entering into the other person's world, suspending our own interpretations and judgements and trying to see things as our clients see them.

Carl Rogers, in his book *A Way of Being*, put it this way:

> *It means entering the private perceptual world of the other and becoming thoroughly at home in it. It involves being sensitive, moment by moment, to the changing felt meanings which flow in this other person, to the fear or rage or tenderness or confusion or whatever that he or she is experiencing. It means temporarily living in the other's life, moving about in it delicately without making judgements. (p. 142)*

It is the process of communicating our empathy to our clients that makes this form of listening active and involving. Effective therapist responses, those that enable clients to feel understood and encouraged to explore more deeply, have some or all of these characteristics:

Accuracy: The therapist must be saying something that accurately captures at least some of the content of the client's words.

Example:

> **Client:** *My sister and I have never got on. I've always been jealous of her, especially when my mother bought her all the best things and I got hand-me-downs. I'm glad she's moved away now, I could never compete anyway.*
>
> **Therapist:** *There was always trouble between you and your sister. You feel better now you don't have to live with her.*

Accuracy and basic empathy: The therapist's response shows an understanding of the more easily accessible feelings and meanings, especially the emotional meanings, of the client's inner world at that time.

Example:

> **Client:** *(same as above)*
>
> **Therapist:** *It must have been hard, feeling second best like that, not cared for as much as her. It seems a relief now, to be free of that.*

Deeper empathy: The therapist is sensing more than just surface meanings and emotions. There is an awareness of the client's feelings that may be lying just below the surface, and the therapist is able to respond to and explore them.

Example:

> **Client:** *I often feel that I have missed out on so much. I mean, I love my kids and everything, but I've had to work so hard to get things for them. When I look back to my childhood there wasn't much fun, not many good times when I could just be carefree. I've tried to make sure life isn't like that for them, but I never got much of anything - it was all work and worry, still is.*
>
> **Therapist:** *It sounds like you never got the kind of childhood you want for your own kids. It's like you missed out on the joy of just being a kid, having fun. I guess it feels like quite a big gap there.*

There have been a number of scales developed to describe and measure the level of empathy present in a therapeutic relationship, some of them quite complex. A simplified, four point scale can be used as a guide to the quality of empathy, and you can use it to check your own responses in a practice session. This scale is adapted from Mearns and Thorne's *Person-Centred Counselling in Action*:

> **Level 0** No evidence of understanding of the client's expressed feelings. May be irrelevant, judgemental, hurtful or rejecting.
>
> **Level 1** Partial understanding of surface feelings. Sometimes called 'subtractive' because the listener has lost something of the client's experience in the response fed back.

Level 2 Shows understanding and acceptance of feelings and thoughts (See *accuracy and basic empathy* above).

Level 3 Shows understanding beyond the level of the client's immediate awareness. Communicates comprehension of surface feelings and *underlying* feelings. Sometimes called 'additive empathy', or *depth reflection* (See *deeper empathy* above).

Tentativeness: The therapist is sensitive and exploratory. He or she isn't diagnosing or interpreting, but checking the extent to which understanding is developing.

Economy: Therapist responses are economical when they communicate directly, and do not include lengthy explanations or descriptions. Being economical is a skill that can be developed using metaphors, similes or figures of speech, for example, to express complex things briefly and understandably.

Example:

Client: *It feels like no matter what I do, I never get anywhere. I try and try, but I make no impression. I seem to put so much time and energy in, but it gets nowhere, all I end up with is a headache* (laughs). *There is a funny side to it, keeping on and on struggling like this, bashing my head against a brick wall, I feel dazed by it.*

Therapist: (with warmth and humour) *Like a woodpecker on a concrete post.*

Client: (Laughs, then seriously) *Yes, exactly, you can imagine how* that *must feel!*

Warmth: The therapist communicates respect and a prizing of the client as unique, worthwhile and to be valued, but please remember what we said earlier about "warmth" not necessarily being the same thing as "affection", and it does not include being over-friendly.

Rapport: The therapist's way of communicating matches the ways in which the client communicates - they "speak the same language", use similar voice tones, and sit in similar ways. Establishing rapport is a matter of being sensitive to the client's way of being and respecting and valuing it. This does not mean, however, that you should mimic your clients, or adopt their words and way of speaking!

Immediacy: The therapist is able to use the present situation, the existing feelings within the client and within him or herself as part of the process of establishing a dialogue with the client. Present, here and now feelings are not denied or avoided, but talked about openly and appropriately.

Example

> **Client:** *I have always had trouble with people I see as being in authority, people with some power over me. I find it really hard to talk to them without feeling small or stupid. I feel it with you sometimes. I'm feeling like that now a bit, and it really annoys me, that I still haven't got over that.*
>
> **Therapist:** *So, for a long time it's been hard to meet people who might put you down, or something, and even with me that feeling comes up, and I guess you might be saying: "Why haven't I grown out of that?"*

In other approaches to psychotherapy, particularly psychodynamic ones, this exchange would be seen as an example of transference. In other words, the client is behaving towards the therapist in ways that are derived from past experiences with others, without being conscious of it. In Person-Centred therapy such feelings or behaviours are not treated any differently from other feelings and behaviours.

Purposefulness: Therapy is more than a conversation - it is a genuine exploration of meanings and experiences. Good therapists are concentrated and focussed. They don't drift off into rambling and meandering small talk.

Blocks to communication

No matter how hard we try to listen attentively, actively and empathically, there often seem to be things which interfere with this process, when we suddenly realise that for a while we have not been listening very well at all. It is difficult to maintain a high level of empathy for long periods of time. Even the most experienced therapists occasionally find their attention wandering, or misunderstanding what someone has said to them.

Empathy is a vital component of good therapy, but we can take great comfort from the fact that often the genuine attempt to understand, even if we don't quite make it, is enough for clients to feel taken seriously, valued and encouraged.

It is also true that *too much empathy* can sometimes be felt as a bit intrusive, even threatening. To have the feeling that someone understands you as well as, if not better than yourself, can for some people be an uncomfortable experience. Empathy is something that good therapists use with sensitivity and care. It has been said that empathy is a bit like garlic - a little goes a long way, too much can be overpowering!

EXERCISE 1: Listening

Aims of the exercise
To understand more about how you listen to people.

What to do
Before going any further with this chapter, take some time to think about ways in which you normally listen to people. Recall situations in which you haven't really understood what was being said. What was happening within you at the time? Were you thinking of something else, trying to win an argument, thinking about what you should say next? Now think of occasions when someone has been listening to you. What was it about their behaviour that helped you feel understood, or not? When you felt misunderstood, what feelings arose in you? Try to remember when you felt clearly understood by someone important to you. What feelings did that experience stimulate in you?

Make a list of behaviour which helped you feel understood. In the past, people have come up with ideas like: "She looked straight at me and nodded from time to time", " She didn't seem distracted by things happening outside", "The things she said back were to the point, connected with what I was trying to say," "She didn't interrupt all the time."

When you have finished these two exercises, compare your ideas with the checklist that follows and see how many of them you experience when trying to be more empathic.

CHECKLIST 4: BLOCKS TO EMPATHY

Being preoccupied
No matter how hard you try, you cannot stop thinking about something else. It might be an important engagement later that day, a letter you have to write, or it might even be a continuous worrying about how empathic you are being!

Being defensive
Your client may be challenging your competence, and you find you begin to justify yourself, or you might simply be worried that your client sees you as someone of less competence than they expected. This, and similar things, can sometimes lead to therapists becoming closed and defensive, which always interferes with their ability to listen.

Being over-sympathetic
Clients sometimes tell us about very unhappy, even tragic events in their lives. If we find ourselves becoming too sympathetic, it can lead us into trying to reassure or make things better. When this happens, we cease to listen properly, and we may become over-concerned with our own emotional state. It may be necessary to be congruent here, and share our sympathetic feelings with our clients. This often enables us to return to the form of listening in which we are able to hear the other person more clearly.

Feeling dislike
If we feel antipathy towards a client, we probably won't be able to listen with acceptance and without judgement. We should explore what it is about this client that leads us to feeling this way. If, as time goes by, we find ourselves still actively disliking this client, we have met a personal limitation. It is honest and professional to admit this, and that we may have to cease giving therapy to this person.

Identifying

Identifying sometimes happens when clients talk about experiences that are familiar to us. We begin to recall these experiences and the feelings that went with them. This is natural, but the danger is in assuming that because we felt a certain way, this client must be feeling the same way, and we begin to relate to clients as if they are having these feelings.

Feeling uncomfortable, shocked or embarrassed

Sometimes clients need to talk about very intimate things, or things that lie quite outside our own experience. This can be particularly true when it comes to talking about sex or sexuality. If clients detect that we are uncomfortable talking about these things, they may try and protect us, and themselves, by avoiding them, which can mean that important therapeutic opportunities are missed.

In training, therapists should confront issues which are personally difficult for them so that their discomfort does not lead to them being unable to listen openly to clients in the future.

The need for reward

We all need to feel that we are doing a good job, really making a positive difference to our clients in helping them lead more satisfying lives. Paradoxically, the need to be a good therapist can become so strong that we try too hard and become anxious, and this affects our capacity to relax and listen.

This can also happen if we have an overpowering need to be liked and respected by our clients.

Forming theories

It can be very tempting to pay more attention to your own process of forming theories about clients than actually to listening to them. Theories might include speculations about how "disturbed" this person is, whether the client has had a very unhappy childhood, whether the client is telling the truth or not, and so on. It is much more productive to attend to your clients' descriptions of themselves, and let them tell you, gradually, what is troubling them, than it is to jump to

31

conclusions. One danger of theories is that you might start believing they are true, and then you might start to relate to your clients as if you knew the truth about them when the chances are that you don't.

Now we have reviewed some of the things that interfere with our ability to listen, we can concentrate on ways of developing more empathic listening behaviour. Some of the exercises that follow are tried and tested ways of focusing on listening with more understanding and insight; others are aimed at developing the communication skills we need to make our empathy known to our clients.

Use the exercises as ways of introducing yourself to the kinds of skills, attitudes and qualities that add up to effective psychotherapy.

EXERCISE 2: Developing empathy - the empathy lab

Aims of the exercise
To develop skills in active, empathic listening by experimenting with a variety of ways of listening and responding.

What to do
This needs three people - a talker, a listener and an observer. The talker and listener should sit opposite each other, and the observer should sit close by, but out of the direct line of sight of the talker and listener so as not to distract them.

The talker should speak of something that has some real meaning. It needn't be a problem, though it could be. The important thing is not to make something up, but to talk about some real experience or feeling. For example, you could talk about your relationships at home, or at work, or about something you did recently that made an impression on you, like visiting somewhere new, or meeting new people.

The listener should try to listen as actively and attentively as possible. Try to listen for meanings which might not be too clear at first. Become aware of the emotions and feelings in the talker's voice. Ask yourself: "What is this person saying to me, and what does it mean for him?"

Try to show the talker that you are really listening and trying to understand, by paraphrasing and summarising what you have heard.

If you don't understand something the talker says, you can ask for it to be repeated, or expressed in different words.

When you have made some kind of response to the talker, allow yourself and the talker some time - it can be difficult to be comfortable with silences, but they are important. Giving someone your full attention like this may seem a bit awkward at first, maybe even a bit mechanical, but as you become more used to it you will find it easier. Eventually, you will find it becomes second nature to listen with greater attention.

Notice how you interfere with your own listening - how you drift off sometimes and miss something, how you find yourself getting a response ready, how you sometimes get some thought triggered off and follow that instead of listening, and so on.

The observer should look at the way the listener pays attention. Does the listener maintain good contact with the talker? What is the listener's body language like? Are the listener's responses accurate, or off the mark? Are they tentative and exploratory, or dogmatic?

Try this, at first, for five or ten minutes. Then debrief with the talker saying how well understood he or she felt, and how well listened to. Try to be as specific as you can in your feedback: "I felt very well understood when you nodded and said...", or, "I don't think you understood me when you said...", or "When you yawned and looked out of the window I didn't feel you were really with me!"

The observer can take notes during the exercise, and be ready to give feedback to the listener, *not* to the talker!

Then swap roles and go through the exercise again. When everyone has had a turn at each role, you can increase the time from five or ten minutes to fifteen or twenty; half an hour is long enough.

The observer will find it helpful to have a short checklist as a reminder of things to look for, and to help with giving the feedback:

The listener:

1. Gives full attention most of the time   **YES/NO**

2. Maintains appropriate eye contact most of the time   **YES/NO**

3. Paraphrases well   **YES/NO**

examples:

    a)

    b)

    c)

    d)

4. Summarises content well   **YES/NO**

examples:

    a)

    b)

    c)

    d)

5. Reflects feelings accurately   **YES/NO**

examples:

    a)

    b)

    c)

    d)

6. Shows empathy   **YES/NO**

examples:

    a)

    b)

    c)

    d)

7. Uses metaphors well   YES/NO

examples:

   a)

   b)

   c)

   d)

8. Summarises feelings well   YES/NO

examples:

   a)

   b)

   c)

   d)

9. Responds tentatively   YES/NO

examples:

   a)

   b)

   c)

   d)

10. Responds economically   YES/NO

examples:

   a)

   b)

   c)

   d)

To develop the skills on the checklist further, try the following exercises.

EXERCISE 3: Using a tape recorder

Aim of the exercise
A variation on the empathy lab. Adds an extra dimension to the feedback and discussion.

What to do
You can use a tape recorder in an empathy lab instead of, or as well as, an observer. The tape will enable you to check specific incidents, and will help you to examine your listening behaviour much more accurately. Tape record an empathy lab and when you play it back, stop it from time to time and recall what you were feeling as the listener, what was going on inside. You might be able to say to the talker: "When you were saying that, I was feeling a bit lost and confused", for example, and you can discuss what effect it might have had if you had shared that feeling with the talker - and possibly explore the reasons you chose not to share it.

EXERCISE 4: Paraphrasing

Aim of the exercise
To develop better communication skills by practising paraphrasing.

What to do
Decide, with a partner, who is to be the talker, and who is to be the listener. The talker speaks about something that has some importance, feelings about a recent incident, a problem at work, for example. The listener should, every couple of minutes, try to paraphrase as briefly as possible what has been said. At first, paraphrasing can seem a bit mechanical and unreal, but remember, it is an exercise in listening and showing you have heard and understood your partner.

Here's an example:

Talker: *This Christmas I had quite a good time with my family. I got some good presents, but the one I liked most was a small framed water-colour from my kids.*

36

It wasn't expensive, but it showed they had put a lot of time into choosing it. It is the kind of picture I really like, and it shows they know me quite well. Those kinds of presents mean a lot more to me than expensive things like CD's or computer games.

Listener: *So Christmas went quite well for you this year, and you valued the care people put into things more than how much they're worth.*

Like all skills, paraphrasing is something that gets more natural, and flows more easily with practice.

EXERCISE 5: Using metaphors and similes

Aim of the exercise
To practice being economical with language, and to enhance the communication of empathy.

Metaphors and other figures of speech help us to communicate complicated things in almost visual ways. For example, the complex feelings associated with being lost, without direction, wandering without purpose, seeming to have no meaning, going through life without any real goals, could be summed up by the phrase: "I am a ship without a rudder".

Like paraphrasing and summarising, using metaphors and similes can feel quite awkward at first, especially if your normal use of language does not include many of them. You have to experiment and find your own style. The important thing is for it to feel and be natural for you. There can be nothing worse than a well meant metaphor sounding out of place or clichéd.

What to do
Make a list of common metaphors or similes that express feelings and emotions, for example:

Leaving no stone unturned

Like banging your head against a brick wall

Like a straw in the wind

Like a dog with two tails

Like a broken record

She was the cat who had the cream

Whenever you hear a new metaphor or simile that seems to sum up a feeling or emotion accurately and sensitively, make a note of it. Use them more freely in your everyday language until they become much more a natural part of it.

EXERCISE 6: Experiencing empathy yourself

Aim of the exercise
To learn to appreciate the power of empathy first hand.

What to do
Of all the ways we know to learn to be more empathic, being deeply understood ourselves is the best. Being a client with an understanding, empathic therapist, or spending time with a naturally empathic friend is a very enriching experience. It teaches us how valuable empathy is in any good relationship, and this somehow triggers off our own empathic abilities. If you do want to be a counsellor or therapist, perhaps you could consider going into therapy yourself.

EXERCISE 7: Empathy in everyday life

Aim of the exercise
To incorporate more empathic understanding in all relationships.

What to do
Next time you are with someone, especially if you care for them, try and listen to them with more attention. Try and put aside your own thoughts and needs and concentrate instead on really trying to understand this person in a new way. This will involve you in trying to sense what life is like for them, and to see things through their eyes. Try and let them know that you have understood them, or at least are trying to understand them more deeply. You may find qualities in them that you had not noticed before, and you may be surprised at how much richer the relationship becomes. This is especially important, and often very rewarding, with children.

Next time you are with someone you dislike, or cannot feel any warmth for, try and put aside the feelings that come up. Try to listen as if it were for the first time, and you may find things in the other person that you can warm towards, or at least you may begin to understand more about why you feel such dislike!

EXERCISE 8: Using transcripts

Aim of the exercise
To practice giving good therapeutic responses to clients.

What to do
Sometimes training courses provide transcripts of therapeutic interviews, or you can find them in books and journals. There are a number in *Client-Centred Therapy*, and *On Becoming a Person*. Read what the client has said, and then, before you read the therapist's response, try and imagine what you might have said had you been the therapist. Imagine that you are sitting in front of this client, hearing these things. What do you feel about what the client said? How would you have responded? Write it down, or use a tape recorder.

Check your responses against what the therapist actually said. Notice the different things that different people focus on, and the variety of ways in which the same statements can be heard and understood. You may find your responses better or worse, although that is not the main aim of this exercise. This exercise can sometimes feel too mechanical or contrived, but it can also be a useful way into thinking about what therapy involves.

EXERCISE 9: Doing it all wrong

Aim of the exercise
To experience the frustration of bad listening.

What to do
This can be quite fun, but it also has a serious side to it. Get into an empathy lab, but this time, instead of listening well and responding well, do everything you can to show you are NOT listening. Look out of the window, yawn a lot, fall

asleep if you can, make up ridiculously inappropriate responses, give a lot of very bad advice. This exercise often leads to a lot of laughter, which is often helpful. It certainly shows up the differences between being listened to and not listened to.

EXERCISE 10: Listening to yourself

Aim of the exercise
To become more aware of your own internal communication.

What to do
Empathy involves a sensitive awareness to the feelings and emotions of others. One way of putting it is that it's like "listening between the lines". How well do you listen to yourself? How often are you really aware of your own feelings?

Take some time to listen to yourself between the lines. In different situations try and become more aware of the variety of feelings you experience as they flow through you. You can try this when you are with someone you like or love, or when you feel yourself to be in a difficult or stressful situation.

A good experience is to find somewhere secluded and put on a favourite piece of music. As the music plays, pay attention to the feelings that come up and say them to yourself: "Now I feel warm and calm like on a quiet beach in the sunshine, now I feel disturbed like I'm expecting something to happen, now I feel sadness..." and so on. It's important that you name the feelings as you become aware of them so you really notice them and acknowledge them.

The more empathic you can be with yourself, the easier you will find it to be empathic with others.

Congruence

It is much more difficult to talk of skills or guidelines when it comes to congruence. In the psychodynamic tradition, therapists need to have their own therapy to become aware of their own resistances, personal needs and problems. This process enables them to be aware of their own feelings towards others, and to make sure they are not confusing their needs with those of their clients.

In Person-Centred therapy it is also necessary for therapists to be as clear as possible in their relationships with clients. Personal, unresolved issues are always present in all of us, but they are less likely to become intrusive if we have spent some time on our own personal growth and psychological health. The best way to do this is through our own therapy, and this also has the advantage of letting us know what it feels like to be a client.

Being aware of our feelings towards others is one aspect of congruence. Another is the ability to communicate in ways that reveal us as people, not as just experts or technicians. If we are to be authentic we can't hide behind roles or masks. We have to come out into the open and meet others openly and non-defensively. This can be quite a hard thing to do, and often it takes some courage to reveal ourselves and our feelings.There is no "how to do it" rule book. It is part of our preparation as therapists to gain the courage and ability to express ourselves in ways that can make us feel a bit vulnerable. Congruence isn't something that happens overnight, but we don't need to be a hundred per cent congruent (even if that were possible), before we can be effective therapists. The development of congruence is a process, probably a life long one that we need to nurture. The more authentic we can become, the more we are able to offer our clients the quality of presence we mentioned earlier.

Exercises in congruence

Technically, congruence is much more than just being aware of feelings, though this is definitely part of it. In a later section, we talk more about "the fully functioning person", and you might find it helpful to read this section now.

EXERCISE 11: Say how you felt

Aims of the exercise

To explore how congruent you are, and to practice expressing congruence.

What to do

This needs two people. Recall a recent event that had some meaning for you. It might be an argument or disagreement with a loved one, or a difficult situation at work - anything that made an impression on you.

As you go through the story, try to be as clear as you can about what you were feeling at the time, and how you feel about it now. Go a little further than you would normally; instead of saying "I felt angry", say what it was in particular that made you angry, and say what you feel about anger itself. Do you have difficulty in expressing anger, for example, or do you get angry easily?

Also, notice more about the people in your story. Do they remind you of others from your past? For example, do you get angry more easily with some kinds of people than others? Why do you think this might be?

Example:

"The more I tried to talk to my doctor about what was wrong with me, the more ir-ritated and angry I got. What really made me angry was that he hardly looked at me. All he did was scribble things down on a pad, and look at his watch. I tried to keep cool, but he hardly seemed to be listening to me at all. At one point I wanted to throw something at him, but I didn't. He reminded me of my Maths teacher at school. I would do the best I could, but he used to treat me as if I didn't exist, he wrote me off as useless. I would try and tell him that I didn't understand, but he couldn't care less. Whenever I get that feeling now, that someone is writing me off, I want to shout, but I never do, in case I get into trouble, I suppose."

Whilst you are doing this, your friend or colleague can be practising his counselling skills, helping you to be clearer about your feelings by listening, reflecting and summarising.

EXERCISE 12: Keeping a journal

Aims of the exercise
To become aware of themes and patterns in your life, and to explore them.

What to do
Keeping a journal can be a powerful way of helping you notice more about yourself. Keep a record of people and events and concentrate on recalling and describing what you were feeling. It can be useful to include a record of your dreams in your journal, again concentrating on the feelings that were part of the dream.

A journal can be a small notebook that you keep with you to jot things down as they occur to you, or a thick, hard-backed book that you keep up to date, if not every day, then at least once a week.

Don't restrict yourself only to writing things. Make sketches or drawings as well. You can also keep pictures and stories that mean something to you from papers or magazines, for example. The point is to keep a record of the changes you notice in yourself, and others around you, and the way you feel you are developing more awareness of yourself. After keeping the journal for some weeks or months you will begin to notice themes and patterns that you were unaware of before.

Keeping a record of dreams can be difficult, because dreams are so easily forgotten very quickly. One way to overcome this is to keep by your bed a small notebook and pencil that you can reach easily in the dark. Whenever you wake up with a dream in your mind, stay still for a moment or two and recall as much detail of the dream as you can, only then should you write down as much as you can remember.

After a few weeks or more you might discover common themes and patterns in your dreams, and it is worth exploring what they might mean to you.

EXERCISE 13: Meditation

Aims of the exercise
To become more familiar with your inner life.

What to do
There are many different forms of meditation and many of them help you to become more aware of your whole self: body, mind, emotions and spirit. Even if you don't want to meditate regularly, it is often useful to spend a little time on your own, sitting or lying comfortably, concentrating on the way you feel at that moment, just letting the feelings develop and come and go without interfering with them or censoring them in any way.

However, if you do want to do meditation, you will find it better if you set aside the same time each day, in the morning or evening, and get into a regular pattern. Choose a place where you won't be disturbed for up to half an hour or more, and make sure the room is warm and that you are sitting or lying comfortably. Sitting cross-legged on the floor is the classic position, but many people find this uncomfortable, at least at first. Lying down is just as good, the important thing is to be comfortable and relaxed.

There are many forms of meditation, but for the purposes of this exercise we suggest that you simply allow your mind to do whatever it wants to do. Spend a few minutes at the start noticing your breathing pattern, and work towards taking regular, fairly deep breaths. Breathe into the whole of your lungs, filling them up from the lower part of your chest by pushing out your abdomen slightly. At the end of your intake of breath, raise your shoulders slightly (as if you were shrugging your shoulders) to allow the air to fill all of your lungs. Hold your breath for a moment or two, then exhale slowly, either through your mouth or nose, whichever is most comfortable. Pause again for a moment or two before taking in another breath.

When you feel you have established a regular breathing pattern, take notice of the way your body feels. Don't try to change anything, just become more aware of any aches or pains.

Now allow your mind to wander, giving it free reign - don't censor anything. You may find your mind settling on particular issues or events. Notice what they are, but again, don't try to direct anything. You can get to know the way your mind works quite well if you do this regularly, say three or four times a week, and you may find that your mind invents some new and creative ways of dealing with problems - but you shouldn't see meditation as a problem-solving exercise.

EXERCISE 14: Guided and self-directed fantasy

Aims of the exercise
More exploration of inner life.

What to do
Everyone has a fantasy life in which we imagine ourselves doing or saying things we would not do in reality. Fantasies can provide useful information about ourselves in a safe, non-threatening way. Many fantasies are sexual ones which we generally keep to ourselves, but there are other kinds that are more easily shared.

You can work with a friend or colleague where you take it in turns to imagine and describe some scene or situation for each other, and then talk through the feelings that came up during it, or you can imagine your own fantasy in which you actually do what you couldn't do in reality - destroying a noisy neighbour's stereo system, telling your boss to jump in a lake, telling someone you love them or hate them. Try to be aware of what it would feel like if you really could do those things. It will help if you can explore them with a friend or colleague.

You will find it useful to write down your fantasies in your journal, if you keep one, and this will help to show themes and patterns that develop with time.

EXERCISE 15: Non-verbal communication

Aims of the exercise
To develop awareness of congruent and incongruent behaviour in yourself and others.

What to do
One thing to be aware of in communication is the extent to which a person's verbal and non-verbal communication match up. Remember, it isn't necessarily because they are lying that people's behaviour doesn't always seem appropriate to what they are saying.

Try to observe people's behaviour more closely when they speak. If someone is saying he feels comfortable and relaxed, why does he keep fidgeting and looking out of the window? If he says he is not angry, why is he raising his voice and tearing up bits of paper?

This is all to do with how much people's feelings are reflected in their observable non-verbal (and verbal) behaviour. If you are in a group, you can ask for feedback and observations from others about how far your behaviour matches what you say you are feeling.

Understanding more about your own non-verbal behaviour is a good place to start. When you are with a client or in a practice session with a colleague, you may feel you are getting tense or vaguely uncomfortable, for example. The signals your body is sending you can help you get clearer about how you are feeling emotionally. A word of warning though. People's behaviour is complex and contains many layers of meaning. It is not easy to tell what someone is really feeling just by watching what he does.

Unconditional positive regard

Unconditional positive regard is a matter of personal values and attitudes rather than a skill or a single piece of behaviour. Our acceptance of our clients is communicated by our way of being with them, rather than by anything in particular we may say or do. If we feel judgemental, we are likely to be judgemental, no matter how much we try to hide it, and hiding our judgementalism would conflict with our aim of being congruent.

Unconditional positive regard does not mean that we have to adopt an attitude of being "nice", or over friendly, or behaving in any way that is false. To do this would be a therapeutic disaster. It probably does make the process easier if we like our clients as people, and even feel great affection for them, but it is not a *condition* of therapy that you *must* like everybody. It is true that there are some people who we like on first sight, with others it may take longer, or it may not happen at all.

It is worth remembering that we care about our clients as people in the process of change, rather than about examples of their behaviour or presently held attitudes. If we find our acceptance or positive regard is conflicting with our congruence, it is probably better that we remain congruent, though this does not have to involve transforming our feelings into negative judgements of our clients as persons.

We all know of people whose behaviour and attitudes we deplore, and we may feel we could never be their therapist because we would always be feeling judgemental about them, or even actively disliking them. This is something we must all consider very carefully. Could you be a therapist to someone you knew to be a child abuser, for example? If you couldn't, what would you do if a client revealed him or herself as one?

Yet often it is the very people about whom we feel most judgemental who need our help, or someone's help, more than anyone. In our experience, people who have done terrible things have themselves experienced terrible things being done to them. Later in this book we talk about "conditions of worth", and you will find that this section helps with unconditional positive regard, which at first sight appears to be an impossible thing to ask of anyone, including Person-Centred therapists.

Exercises to explore unconditional positive regard

Unconditional positive regard is an attitude or set of values towards others that cannot be directly taught or learned. We are all influenced, in some way or another, to be able to accept some things about people more easily than others. And we have probably all internalised attitudes towards others that, on closer examination, turn out to be irrational or founded more on prejudice than reality.

Our early experiences with people are very powerful in shaping the kinds of attitudes we hold, and often we are quite unconscious of our prejudices. It is possible to spend some time revealing our own prejudices, likes and dislikes, and seeing how far we need to hold on to the prejudices we have and the stereotypes we have unconsciously made a part of ourselves.

EXERCISE 16: Stereotype bashing

Aims of the exercise
To explore what unconditional positive regard means for you. To test the limits of your positive regard. To develop more awareness of yourself and others. To examine stereotyping and prejudice.

What to do
As it is very important in Person-Centred therapy to be able to deal with issues of power openly, it is crucial that therapists confront and deal with their own racism, sexism and other prejudices.

All good training courses include the examination of racist and sexist attitudes and help would-be therapists to overcome them. You can supplement this by going on good racism and sexism awareness workshops, and by really paying attention to the attitudes and values you hold.

In the meantime, you can start the process yourself by becoming more aware of some of the stereotypes and prejudices you hold, and by beginning to re-examine them. The first thing is not to be afraid of being prejudiced or to view it as a matter of shame, but you need to be open to change and to re-evaluating the views and opinions you hold about people.

Stereotyping happens because it is too complicated to see everything in individual terms, and we need general categories to help us make sense of all the complexities of human life. It obviously isn't helpful in therapy, though, to hang on to stereotypes that prevent us from seeing people as individuals, with unique experiences, feelings and needs, even though they seem to be members of particular groups.

Prejudices arise mainly through fear of the unknown or fear of differences that we don't understand. They are often composed of subtle, (and not so subtle), messages that have become taken for granted, and passed on in attitudes, media images, "jokes" and stories. Write down a list of groups and "types", like :

Women, black people, Muslims, Scottish people, Irish people, Jews, Catholics, disabled people, English people, football supporters, teenagers, the elderly, Americans, northerners, men, southerners.

Next to each heading, write down a list of words or phrases that come immediately into your mind, for example :

Americans: rich, hospitable, superficial, violent, consumers, overweight, meat eaters, warm, fitness fanatics, "have a nice day", friendly, creative.

English people: cool, reserved, stiff, unfriendly, inefficient, conservative, repressed, sincere, inventive, cultured.

When you've got as complete a list as you can manage, share and compare it with a partner's list, preferably someone in a different "group" from yourself. You will probably find that some of the words in your list contradict each other, like "overweight" and "fitness fanatics". Explore the words and phrases against each of the headings. How many of them are actually true as far as you can see, and how many of them are clearly prejudices, biases and stereotypes?

EXERCISE 17: Valuing yourself

One way to become more accepting of others is to become more accepting of yourself. What parts of you do you dislike, or would like to change for the better?

Do you have a healthy level of self-esteem, do you value the good things about yourself?

Do you blame yourself for your imperfections? Do you find it easy to forgive yourself when you do something you dislike or regret later?

Many of us find it easier to admit to our faults and the things we don't like about ourselves, than to acknowledge and value our good, positive sides. This exercise is designed to focus on your positive, creative and likeable characteristics, and to admit to them and share them with others.

Aims of the exercise
To learn to appreciate and value your positive characteristics.

What to do
Write down: Ten things I really value about myself.

For example:

> I really value the way I talk to my kids.
>
> I really value the way I can entertain people.
>
> I really value the way I listen to people.
>
> I really value the way I care about the people close to me.
>
> I really value my sense of humour.

You can now share your list with a partner or with your group. Learn to recognise and appreciate the positive things in yourself, they are what you build on in your relationships with others, including your clients.

EXERCISE 18: Making judgements
Sometimes, when we are quick to make judgements about others, it turns out that the things we dislike in them are the same things we dislike in ourselves. When you find yourself being judgemental, ask yourself: "What is it about this person that reminds me of things I dislike in myself?" This process of seeing in others elements of ourselves is sometimes called "projection".

Aims of the exercise
To become aware of some ways in which we project parts of ourselves onto others.

What to do
Write down a list of people you dislike or feel wary of. They may be people you know personally, or people you have heard about through others. Next to each name, write down the things about them that you dislike or make you feel uncomfortable.

Now, with a partner or group, look closely at the list you have made, and talk through the ways in which you might also have some of those characteristics.

Alternatively, write down as much detail as you can about someone who makes you feel uncomfortable. Either role-play that person yourself with your group and talk afterwards about what it felt like to be that person, or have another member of your group role-play the person as a client for whom you are the therapist. Again, talk through what it felt like to be that person's therapist, and how you might try to see beyond the dislikeable characteristics to other aspects of the person.

EXERCISE 19: Things from the past
Sometimes we find ourselves disliking particular kinds of people, though rationally there seems to be no good reason why this should be so. It may be that some people remind us, in some way, of unhappy experiences we once had, and those experiences can get "restimulated" without us being fully aware of it. The process of behaving towards people in the present in ways that are derived from our past experiences (without us being conscious of this), is sometimes referred to as "transference".

Aims of the exercise
To bring some of the past into the present, and to become aware of how we might relate to people today based on past experiences.

What to do
Think of groups of people you dislike and write down the specific things about them you imagine to be so dislikeable. For example:

Police officers, because they are too powerful and authoritarian. Doctors, because they never listen to what you say.

Now either write down, or recount to a partner or group, whatever you can recall from your past experiences with these people. Take it in turns to explore incidents, memories, vague impressions and more vivid memories. Concentrate especially on what you felt while these things were taking place, and notice how far you have extended characteristics that might have been true about an individual person to include the whole group he or she represents.

EXERCISE 20: Hurt people do hurtful things
Something for all therapists to remember is that people who themselves have experienced great hurt often turn out to do hurtful and destructive things to others. This does not mean that we have to condone or excuse their actions, but it does help us to work with such people.

It's also worth remembering that when such people come for therapy they are implicitly recognising their hurtful behaviour and are wanting to do something about it.

Aims of the exercise
To understand how previous hurtful experiences can affect present day behaviour.

What to do
When you next come across someone who behaves in destructive, even violent ways, or whenever you read about such people, ask yourself what kinds of experiences that person might have had as a very young child, that may have led to this behaviour.

For a deep analysis of how painful and destructive experiences in childhood can echo throughout life, read the books by Alice Miller (see the Books section).

Some different approaches

Another way of illustrating the main characteristics of Person-Centred therapy is to look again at some of Jack's statements, but this time to respond to them in very different, non Person-Centred ways.

Client: *Well, there are so many things. I don't know if you can help with them...It just seems that everything gets on top of me so easily these days, much more than they used to. I suppose I have been having a bad time lately. I don't seem to get on with my teenage daughter like I used to....I feel very unhappy at work, maybe I've been there too long. My wife and I seem to be at each other's throats...I don't know.. coming to a therapist seems like a last resort, but I can't keep going like this much longer.*

Therapist: *You're very tense. I think we should try some relaxation exercises later, you might find them useful at work. Could you say more about your relationship with your daughter?*

Here, the therapist has told Jack how he is feeling, and has suggested a solution to this "problem". The therapist has also begun to direct the therapy by suggesting Jack talk about his daughter.

Client: *I do feel a bit on my own. In fact I feel alone a lot of the time. Because there isn't anything specific, I can't really talk much about it. My wife says I'm moody and closed off... but how do you talk about something and nothing? It all seems a bit futile.*

Therapist: *Your feeling of being alone probably stems from the breakdown of your relationships at home. How does your wife feel about you at the moment... have her feelings for you changed?*

The therapist is really beginning to interpret and diagnose Jack now, then neatly, but unhelpfully, removes Jack from his own feelings and gets him to speculate about the feelings of someone else!

Client: *I just feel like I'm complaining when I have no real right to. I've got every-thing I need....why do I feel so, so unhappy?*

Therapist: *That sounds like an old tape you're playing there. Did your parents say those kinds of things to you? What was your relationship with your parents like?*

This is a bit of Transactional Analysis coupled with more than a hint of Freud. The therapist isn't concentrating on understanding Jack from Jack's point of view, but leading him into a discussion of his childhood. In Person-Centred therapy, Jack will do this when he sees it as important, and in his own way. What this therapist is doing is formulating Jack's problems for him, and suggesting the solution.

Client: *No, it doesn't. I usually just keep these things to myself. Most people would never suspect I feel this way. I know my wife knows I'm unhappy. I think she's a bit scared of it, as if it's something to do with her. I want to tell her it isn't, but if we do start to talk about it we end up rowing, or I deny there's anything wrong.*

Therapist: *People who have difficulty expressing their feelings often feel depressed and unhappy, just like you do. Let's try an experiment. Imagine your wife is in the empty chair next to you, and you are able to talk to her. What is it that you'd really like to say to her? If you practice it here it'll be easier to do it in reality. Would you like to try this for a while?*

The first remark tells the client what is wrong with him. It isn't very accepting or understanding of Jack's present feelings about himself. Next, the therapist takes complete charge. This technique (a Psychodrama and Gestalt technique) may be very useful in some circumstances, but it removes the possibility for Jack to explore his feelings in his own way, developing his own resources, and places responsibility for the therapy squarely on the therapist. In Gestalt psychotherapy this technique would be introduced sensitively as an integral part of an ongoing process, not suddenly and sharply stuck in like this. Jack could decline the invitation, but many clients find it very hard to resist powerful suggestions like this.

Client: *When I think about that, about what I just said, it does feel like there's another person in me, or perhaps it's another bit of me, who has kept quiet for a long time, and not really been happy with what's going on. I mean, the main bit of me is successful and all that, but .... I need to think about this more...*

Therapist: *It seems there are parts of you not very well integrated, sort of split off. Try not to think so much and get more in touch with what you are feeling. Let's try and get acquainted with that quiet person and find out what he wants.*

This response is very interpretive and diagnostic: "You have a split personality"; it would be a very difficult thing for a client to hear and make some sense of. Next, it devalues Jack's need to take time and think, and admonishes him for not being a feeling enough person - very judgemental! Finally, it offers a solution to what the therapist assumes to be the problem.

Other techniques

You will have noticed that we do not describe techniques like relaxation, guided fantasy, or role playing as part of the therapeutic process, though we think such techniques can be useful in developing more awareness of ourselves, in training groups for example. In our experience, Person-Centred therapists tend to use very few techniques like these, if any at all. Carl Rogers' view was that they may be useful only in so far as they help to establish a relationship built on the three core conditions of empathy, congruence and unconditional positive regard.

A problem in Person-Centred therapy (and all other therapies) occurs when the therapist reaches for a technique either when the going gets tough (when the client seems "stuck" for example), or simply because the therapist knows a lot of techniques and wants to use them. It would be better to ask ourselves about the quality of empathy we are giving, the degree to which we are being congruent, and the extent to which we are being judgemental, before opting for a technique that might gloss over these problems.

Techniques are not Person-Centred if they serve to remove the focus of the therapy away from the client's inner world to that of the therapist, or if they divert clients' attention away from what they are presently feeling towards something the therapist thinks they ought to feel. As we said before, Person-Centred therapists take the view that the client is the one and only expert. It is the client who knows what hurts, and it is only the client who has the resources and power for change. The therapist's role is to help provide the conditions of security and trust that enable clients to discover, develop and use their own resources.

CHAPTER FOUR

THEORY AND PHILOSOPHY OF PERSON-CENTRED THERAPY

Carl Rogers first proposed the core-conditions we mentioned previously, in the late 1950's. Originally, he gave six conditions, but three were subsequently thought to be self-evident, and attention focussed on the remaining three. As we have seen, these are:

Therapy is most likely to be effective when:

- therapists experience an empathic understanding of the client's inner world, and communicate that understanding to the client,
- therapists maintain personal congruence in their relationships with clients. Sometimes the words "authenticity" or "realness" are used here,
- therapists experience and communicate unconditional positive regard for their clients. Sometimes words like "warmth" or "acceptance", or "prizing" are used here.

It is the experience of being deeply understood by another person that creates the possibility for change. But why should being understood, without judgement, by a "real" person effect change? For the answer to this, we need to go deeper into Person-Centred philosophy and theory, but first we suggest you take some time to do the following exercise:

EXERCISE 21: Your own philosophy of the person

Aims of the exercise
To explore and describe your currently held philosophy of what it means to be a person.

What to do
Describe your own philosophy of human nature by responding to the statements that follow. If you are doing this in a small group, take about an hour to do the exercise on your own, then compare your ideas with the others in the group. The point is not to anticipate what Person-Centred philosophy is, but to identify and share your own attitudes and ideas.

1. People are basically self-centred and concerned about their own welfare more than that of others.

2. Society needs firm rules and laws to control people who would otherwise exploit the people around them, because this is only human nature.

3. People who become psychologically disturbed are in need of firm but kind help and direction from properly trained experts.

4. We are all social, each of us has needs that cannot be met by remaining isolated from the rest of humanity.

5. God created humankind to hold a privileged position in the world, superior to all else in creation.

6. Everything about people is determined by the material conditions existing around them.

7. The kind of person you are is determined by the kind of society in which you are brought up.

8. Every mental event has a cause. Nothing is ever completely haphazard or accidental.

9. Our consciousness is controlled and shaped by internal forces of which we are not aware.

10. Experiences and events in early childhood create our character which soon becomes fixed and more-or-less unchangeable.

11. Humans were not created for any particular purpose. We just are, and we have to decide what to do about it.

12. There is no limit to personal freedom.

13. Every aspect of our mental lives is intentional, and our sole responsibility. We choose who we are, and how to be.

14. People behave in ways that are determined entirely by their environmental conditions.

15. Our behaviour is subject to the same natural laws that apply to animals.

16. People are basically constructive and social. Destructive behaviour is learned behaviour and results from destructive experiences in childhood.

17. People have the capacity to decide for themselves how they want to change and develop.

18. There's not much you can do to change the way you are once you become an adult. The best thing is to learn to live with it.

19. Normal people never need psychotherapy.

20. Psychological disturbance is like an illness that can be cured with the proper treatment once the cause is known.

The philosophy of the Person-Centred Approach

An existential view of living
Existentialists believe that people arrive at their own view of reality as a result of their own experiences. In other words, each one of us makes sense out of what we experience in personal, idiosyncratic ways. We behave in ways that match our subjective awareness of ourselves and the environment in which we live. Even if objective reality exists it does not determine our behaviour, but the way in which we perceive and make sense of reality does.

While there are many obstacles and limitations to our freedom, we can make worthwhile efforts to overcome them. Humankind is responsible for whatever it has become (and can become), because people can choose, to a significant degree, "how to be".

To be one's own creator (in this limited sense) takes courage, because many of us fear the consequences and responsibilities that such freedom brings with it. To admit that all our values and projects are of our own choosing means we have to take sole responsibility for them. This brings with it a paradox - while we desire freedom, we are also afraid of it.

This is an *existential* philosophy, and it includes the central notion that we are, in many ways, free to choose. Life is not, in other words, determined for us.

Related to this, Rogers' way of understanding human nature was to place great value on striving to appreciate people's personal worlds from within their own frames of reference. He was interested to discover how people made sense from their experience, how they arrived at conclusions about themselves and others, how it felt to be them.

The actualising tendency

Another element in Person-Centred theory is the hypothesis that an *actualising tendency* is universal in all living things, including human beings. By this is meant the assumed inherent capacity for all organisms, no matter what they are, to move towards becoming as fully functioning as possible. In the natural world, an organism will tend to develop its full potential as long as the environmental conditions are suitable for it. It doesn't have to put any conscious effort into this; where the environment is perfectly suitable, the organism will grow and develop naturally.

It is only when there are adverse environmental conditions that the organism will suffer, not develop fully, or become diseased and die unnaturally. But even under adverse environmental conditions the organism will strive to become as fully functioning as the conditions will allow. A plant kept away from the light will still put out shoots that grow and bend towards whatever light is available, even if those shoots are pale and lacking in vigour. This actualising tendency is assumed to be a characteristic of all organic life, and is suggested as the basic motivational force in human development. A part, or sub-system of the actualising tendency is *self-actualisation*.

In other words, there is a general tendency for the organism as a whole to become all of its potential, and, in human beings, what can be thought of as a part of this general trend becomes observable as a tendency to maintain and actualise a "self" or *self concept*.

A common mistake is to believe that Carl Rogers thought that this meant that people were basically "good". In fact, Rogers never said he thought people were "good", because what is good or bad depends very much on your point of view, and the time and culture in which you live. He did sometimes refer to "the good life" by which he meant the more satisfying and fulfilling way of life possible when we can can use more of our potential and express ourselves openly and clearly.

Rogers did think, however, that the actualising tendency was a positive and creative one. He believed that evil or destructive behaviour was a result of childhood experiences and conditioning, and that the process of self-actualisation could be damaged or corrupted, sometimes in very profound ways.

This might become more understandable if we look at the way Person-Centred theory explains the process of human development from birth, and the emergence of a "Self": that which differentiates me from you.

Personality theory
Rogers proposed that infants enter the world in a state of full congruence, and their experiences of their new environment constitute reality for them. Human nature is regarded as essentially constructive, and human beings as motivated to pursue the truth rather than be satisfied with half-truths or deception. Positive self-regard is viewed as a basic human need, and people do their best to develop and protect themselves whatever internal or external circumstances prevail (see: *The Core Values and Theory of the Person-Centred Approach*, by Bozarth and Temaner-Brodley).

In interacting with their environment, infants are motivated by the actualising tendency. Certain experiences will be perceived as satisfying the process of actualisation, and others as being detrimental to actualisation.

Experiences, then, are valued either positively or negatively by the *organismic valuing process*. This is not a conscious activity, though negatively valued experiences will be avoided, and positive ones sought.The experiences of reality for each infant are unique and each develops its own *internal frame of reference* which cannot completely be assumed by another.

As the infant develops, so does an awareness of its "self", which is part of its total experience. It is able to differentiate between its own experience and that of others. One of Rogers' basic theories was that each individual has a strong need for positive regard from the other people on whom it is dependent for survival. This need develops alongside the emergence of the self-concept, and the infant develops a sense of self-regard in accordance with its varied experiences of life.

Because the infant is so dependent for its continued survival on others, the organismic valuing process can be overridden by the need for positive regard from them. Put another way, the infant's organismic valuing process is vulnerable to the overwhelming need to be accepted, protected and nurtured by others. The infant will, therefore, begin to adopt values from outside of itself and internalise them in an effort to maintain the support and nurturing it needs to survive. The infant's trust in its own experiencing and valuing is likely to become suppressed if it conflicts with the values and needs of others more powerful than itself.

Infants thus acquire *conditions of worth*. They learn from experience that they are only acceptable as long as they think, feel and behave in ways that are positively valued by others. They seek certain kinds of experiences, and avoid others, according to how far they fit these acquired conditions of worth. Experiences and feelings that match these conditions of worth are perceived accurately and are accepted, but those that are contrary to them are distorted or denied completely. This process can be thought of as the beginnings of psychological maladjustment, when there is a state of *incongruence* existing between "self" and experience.

If we go back to our client, Jack, for a moment, we can get some inkling of one of his conditions of worth when he says:

Client: *Yes, I've always believed you should be happy with what you've got, there are so many worse off....I mean I'm not starving or in the middle of a war or anything. It's so hard to talk about this....it would almost be better if I did have some big issue that I could point to and say, this is what's making you unhappy, but there isn't anything.... it all feels a bit phoney, making a mountain out of a molehill.*

This could easily indicate to us that one of the messages Jack received when he was young was: "It's not OK to be unhappy when there are so many worse off than you." Jack would have found it difficult to express negative feelings without also feeling guilty or anxious in some way.

When, as often happens, a person continues to experience something that is not consistent with the self-structure, including its conditions of worth, this experience is felt as threatening. An example of this might be when a child experiences anger towards a parent or brother or sister. It may be that the expression of anger is met with disapproval, punishment or the withholding of love. The child learns that anger is unacceptable and this becomes internalised as a condition of worth: "I am not acceptable when I am angry". In the future, when anger begins to be felt again, the person is likely to suppress the feeling, deny it, or distort it into something more acceptable.

This is where defences come from. A defence is the process of distorting experience, or denying it, so that the experience doesn't threaten the person's self-structure, and is consistent with that person's conditions of worth. The outcome is the cutting off of experience from awareness, or the distortion of it in some way so as to fit the existing self-structure.

The process of internalising conditions of worth results in the emergence not of a true or "organismic" self (that self that would have developed in ideal conditions), but of a false or conditional self. This is the self that operates in the world, and this is the self that the person continues to actualise. Thus, the process of self-actualisation can, in effect, run counter to the positive, growthful direction of the general actualising tendency.

Since all of us have internalised conditions of worth, we all actualise a conditional self. People with many negative conditions of worth will be attempting to actualise a damaged or corrupted "self". This helps to explain how Person-Centred theory accepts the positive, healthy, social potential in each person (the actualising tendency), but at the same time accepts that people's behaviour can be destructive, unhealthy and anti-social (the actualisation of a false or damaged self).

EXERCISE 22: Your conditions of worth

Aims of the exercise

To explore and understand early childhood conditioning. To explore how far conditions of worth affect our present day feelings and behaviour.

What to do

This exercise is designed to help you describe some of the ways in which your conditions of worth developed, and it is best done in the company of an understanding and supportive group. It is not a substitute for your own personal therapy, but it may bring up things for you that you could talk over with a therapist.

Take plenty of time for every member of the group to share whatever they want to share. Nobody should feel pressured into talking about things if they don't feel ready to. A variation of this exercise is to spend some time on your own responding to the prompts given here, then team up with one other person and talk through the things that occurred to each of you. First, respond to the prompts that follow and see if you recognise any of them as messages you received as a child. When you think you are familiar with the kinds of issues we are raising here, add to the list those things you think were around when you were a child.

1. Children should be seen and not heard.

2. Expressing emotions is not OK, especially in company.

3. Big boys don't cry.

4. Being emotional is the same as being weak.

5. Girls are not as important as boys.

6. It is wrong to be angry.

7. There are certain rules to life, and if you don't obey them it's because you are bad.

8. Keep yourself to yourself. It is wrong to let other people know your business.

9. Other people know best.

10. There are always people worse off than you. Be grateful for what you've got.

The goals of therapy

Person-Centred therapy aims to expose and re-evaluate conditions of worth, and return the person to a state of congruence - that state in which feelings can be fully felt, accepted and expressed appropriately, combined with a trust and acceptance of the organismic valuing process.

Put in a warmer, more human way, Person-Centred therapy is a sensitive exploration of a person's inner world, a reliving in a safe and caring relationship of those things that hurt and damaged us. It is the release of constructive energy (energy no longer needed to shore up defences and maintain a false self), to enable the experiencing of the joys and sorrows of life more creatively and more authentically.

The idea of an *internal* rather than *external locus of evaluation* is an important one here. People who have internalised many conditions of worth won't have much faith or trust in themselves, and are unlikely to hold themselves in very high regard. They are likely to look outside themselves, to others, for judgements and evaluations, and are likely to have more faith or belief in those judgements than they do in their own.

A general outcome of successful therapy is a shift away from dependence on the judgements of others, towards a greater trust and belief in the validity of internal judgements. A general goal of psychotherapy might, then, be expressed in terms of helping people to trust the information obtained from their own senses, to value it, and use it as a reliable guideline for determining personal action. We discuss this more in the chapter dealing with "the fully functioning person", and it will help to read this chapter now for a better outline of what therapy hopes to achieve.

A note about transference....

"Transference" refers to attitudes and feelings that have their origins in earlier relationships with parents or others, that become unconsciously "transferred" onto the therapist. In other words, clients begin to relate to their therapists, and to have feelings towards them, in ways which really belong somewhere in the client's past.

In psychodynamic therapy, transferred feelings and attitudes are treated as indicators of unresolved conflicts that exist in the present day but have their origins in the past. Uncovering and working through these transferences is an essential part of the work of the psychodynamic therapist.

Person-Centred therapists, in the main, do not deny the existence of transference, but take a very different attitude towards it in the therapy room. Carl Rogers believed that strong transference relationships were more likely to occur within directive forms of therapy, where clients become dependent on the skill and expertise of the therapist to make interpretations. He believed that such situations were less likely to occur within the Person-Centred Approach and, to him, the concept of transference was much less important.

Rogers thought that working with transference feelings by making them of central importance to the therapeutic process was a mistake. Person-Centred therapy responds to statements from clients which may be transference, in exactly the same way as with all other statements - with empathy, congruence and positive regard.

This is one of the areas in which psychodynamic and Person-Centred therapists part company most obviously. Whereas both agree that the nature of the therapeutic relationship is important, and both agree that accurate, empathic listening is a central skill, they do not agree that one of the main functions of therapy is to stimulate and work through transference feelings.

...and counter-transference

Counter-transference refers to feelings that therapists develop towards clients, which are believed to have their origins in much earlier relationships in the therapist's life. Counter-transference is an unconscious process, and in psychodynamic therapy it is considered very important for therapists to have their own therapy or analysis so that such feelings do not interfere with the therapeutic process. In the Person-Centred Approach too it is very important that therapists are aware of their own psychological histories, and can distinguish between feelings that arise as a result of here and now experiencing, and those that are rooted in their past.

The importance of the therapeutic relationship

The power for positive therapeutic change comes from the actualising tendency - the movement towards wholeness and becoming fully functioning. The therapist tries to provide a relationship with the kind of qualities we have already described to enable the actualising tendency to find expression. If the psychological environment is right, clients can be trusted to discover for themselves, and in their own ways, the resources they need for change and growth. Just like gardeners don't "grow" plants, they grow by themselves, therapists don't "grow" persons. What both the gardener and the therapist try to do is create the conditions in which the inherent capacities for growth and development can come to fruition.

As someone once said: " You have to change by yourself, but you don't have to do it on your own." This reflects the notion that therapy should never contain any element of control or authority exercised by therapists over clients.

Before we leave this brief discussion of theory and philosophy, we give a number of statements which, taken together, provide a summary of Person-Centred theory :

CHECKLIST 5: PERSON-CENTRED THEORY

1. Person-Centred therapy stems from the acceptance that there is an underlying tendency towards fulfilment of all positive potentials - towards greater complexity and wholeness, not just for maintenance of the status quo, but for development and enhancement.

2. People have within themselves great resources for personal change, self-understanding, growth and actualisation. These resources can become available within the context of a therapeutic relationship, the characteristics of which can be defined.

3. Creative and growthful relationships are ones where individual personal power is contacted and expressed, and in which the choice of how to use the relationships remains with clients themselves.

4. Person-Centred therapy offers relationships in which people's felt realities, or inner worlds can be explored from within their own frames of reference, using their own resources, meaning systems and means of expression.

5. Person-Centred therapy enables the sensitive and progressive revealing of layers of meaning and experience that have led to each person's uniqueness and individuality.

6. The Person-Centred therapist aims to contribute to this process by experiencing and communicating empathic understanding of the complex reality of each individual, by prizing, respecting and valuing each individual, and by remaining congruent, open and non-defensive in relationships with clients.

Now we know something more about the theory and philosophy of Person-Centred therapy, it is important we find ways of being with our clients that are *consistent* with that theory and philosophy. It is no good *saying* we trust our clients to find their own resources for change if we are constantly trying to change them ourselves.

EXERCISE 23: Staying with the client

Aims of the exercise
To show how we can unwittingly move away from the client's frame of reference.
To practice ways of responding which stay closer to the client's experiencing.

What to do
Read each of the following client/therapist interactions, and discuss with your group, or think on your own, about how you might have responded. Remember, there is no perfect therapeutic response, but some are more likely to help clients move forward than others, and some might serve to put a complete stop on the proceedings.

1. Imposing values

Client: *I've got myself into so much trouble. My parents don't know I've been sleeping with my boyfriend for some time....we do love each other....but now I'm pregnant. I just don't know what to do for the best....I want to go to college soon, but I couldn't with a baby. I don't know how to tell my Mum, or even if I should.*

Therapist: *Well, you really ought to tell your Mum and Dad, I'm sure they'll understand, parents usually do. You could put off going to college for a while, you're still young enough.*

2. Telling the client what the problem is

Client: *My partner and I just don't talk much any more about anything. We used to talk a lot about things, make decisions together, but these days we just sit in silence most of the time. We don't do much together either. If I don't suggest something, nothing happens. I don't know what's wrong, or how we got like this.*

Therapist: *You've drifted apart, lost touch with each other. This often happens after a few years of living together. You've probably got different interests and ideas now.*

3. Telling clients how they are feeling

Client: *I don't sleep much these days, and I worry about things all the time. I don't seem to have much energy and I don't do half the things I used to. I get bad tempered if anyone tries to get me to do anything. The house is a mess, but I can't bring myself to clean it up. This morning I couldn't even be bothered to take the dog for a walk.*

Therapist: *You're over anxious and depressed - this often happens when people are under some kind of stress.*

4. Giving advice

Client: *My boss is always complaining about me these days. My work isn't any different from anyone else's, but as far as he's concerned I can't do anything right. He picks on me all the time, and it's so unfair. It all seemed to start when he made a pass at me a couple of months ago, and I turned him down.*

Therapist: *You should speak to your Union Officer about it, or think about leaving.*

5. Asking closed questions

Client: *I feel lonely most of the time, even though we have a big family, there are seven of us kids. The others seem to be OK, but I feel out of things most of the time, and do most things on my own. Nobody seems to take much notice of me, and I find myself going my own way most of the time. I'd like to feel more a part of things, but I just don't.*

Therapist: *When did you first notice you were feeling this way?*

6. Asking for more information too soon.

Client: *Since my Mother died, I haven't really felt well in myself. I get nervous about going out, and I don't like meeting new people. I spend most of my time at home, sometimes I don't even answer the phone, not that it rings that much. At weekends I sometimes don't go out of the house at all, and on Monday mornings I feel sick when I have to go to work.*

Therapist: *How long ago did your mother die? Do you have any other family?*

7. Identifying

Client: *Since my marriage broke up I haven't had any interest in any new relationships. I don't go to places where I might meet anyone, I just don't like doing that, and I don't want to do it. My friends say I'm becoming a recluse, that I should get out and meet people, but I can't be bothered.*

Therapist: *I know what you mean. It took me three years to get over my divorce, but like you, I enjoyed being on my own for a while.*

Client: *No, I don't like being on my own, but I don't want to take the risk of being hurt again, or getting into a sexual thing that I can't control.*

Therapist: *Yes, I know. Many people go off sex for a while, I know I did.*

Client: *Well, sex is the one thing I miss most.*

8. Being over-reassuring

Client: *I feel like I must be getting ill with something serious. I keep seeing things, and getting dizzy spells. I'm really afraid of dying. My father died of cancer, and I'm terrified it might be hereditary or something. I keep getting these headaches, and I really feel in a panic.*

Therapist: *I'm sure there's nothing much wrong with you. A lot of people get dizzy spells, and I'm sure cancer isn't passed on.*

9. Being uncomfortable with silences

Client: *I feel very close to some kind of crisis. Maybe it won't be a bad thing, but it feels like some big change is about to happen for me. It scares me quite a bit, it's like I'm anticipating something, but I don't know what it is. I need to spend some time thinking about it, or just being with it, there's not much I can actually say about it.*

(Very short pause)

Therapist: *Do you have any idea what it is?*

10. Blocking Emotions

Client: *I feel really angry with my ex-husband. He's started phoning me up all day and all night. I try to tell him how angry I am about it, but he just won't listen at all. I can feel the anger coming up just talking about him... the way he treated us...*

and now he wants things from me...Jesus... sometimes I feel I could kill him if he does it any more. I'd like to break his neck. If he walked in here now I'd murder him.

Therapist: *Try and relax, and tell me how all this started.*

11. Talking about others

Client: *Every time I see my father, we end up having a big row. Give us two minutes and we're at each other's throats. He's just so closed-minded about everything, and stuck in his ways. I feel like kicking him whenever I see him. It didn't used to be like that, we used to be quite good friends, but I just can't stand the sight of him now. He finds fault in everything I do.*

Therapist: *Maybe your father is as upset by all these rows as you seem to be.*

12. Being analytical

Client: *I just don't seem to be able to find anyone I really like enough to want to be with, other than as a friend. I'd like to find someone special, but I'm very suspicious of most of the men I meet. I mean, they seem all right at first, then it all starts going wrong. I'm afraid I'll end up with someone like my father, always running off and getting drunk. He used to be quite violent sometimes when he drank too much.*

Therapist: *You probably still have unresolved feelings towards your father, and this is why you're still so afraid of men - because they remind you of him in some way.*

COMMENTARY ON THE EXERCISE

We hope the exercise helped you to frame responses that were a little more open, understanding and caring than most of the ones given above. In all of the above responses the therapist is trying to be helpful in some way or another, and the therapist's intention is clearly to help the client go further, or think things through further. The trouble with most of them is that they don't really respect the client's ability to come to his or her own conclusions, and they often serve to close down exploration rather than open it up.

1. This response is an obvious imposition of a set of values which may be miles away from those of the client. In any case, it is not the therapist's job to be

providing value judgements at all. Much better would have been to reflect the various dilemmas this client faces, and help her explore ways in which she might deal with the situation herself.

2. This is a diagnosis of this person's problem. The therapist cannot possibly know what the situation is, or whether these two people have developed other interests or not. The response comes from within the therapist's frame of reference, it does not try to get into the client's shoes at all.

3. This is another diagnosis. According to the therapist the client is stressed, and this explains the problem. There might very well be some stress here, but a much better response would have been a simple reflection of the different feelings the client is having, and not an attempt to generalise the problem.

4. In different circumstances, this might be very good advice. But again, it is not the therapist's job to advise clients about how to solve their problems. Better would have been to help the client explore her feelings about her boss's unwelcome advance and its consequences, and to help the client explore her own strategies for dealing with them.

5. In our training groups we encourage people to try not asking any questions at all, particularly not closed questions like this. Sometimes questions, if they are open and exploratory, are helpful in enabling clients to focus more clearly, but closed questions are hardly ever of any use. Again, it would have been better to try and understand the loneliness, and to offer some understanding of it. This would have had the beneficial effect of the client feeling heard.

6. Asking for more information often brings with it the feeling that the information given so far is somehow not enough, or not valuable enough. There is plenty of feeling in this client's statement so far to be able to understand something of how life is for her at the moment. Better to respond to this with empathy than ask for something else.

One question we would like all therapists to strike from their list would be: "How did that make you feel?" Usually this question comes in response to a statement from the client that was bursting with emotion - but the therapist just did not hear it!

7. This speaks for itself. This therapist identified with the client, and thought he knew how the client must feel. He was wrong, twice.

8. This client's fear of death is real and understandable, particularly as she witnessed her own father's death. The therapist simply ignores this very real fear, and offers something not very helpful at all. To go on now and explore feelings about death and illness would be very difficult for this client; after all, she's been practically told she's making it all up!

It would be a good idea, however, to check out with this client at some appropriate point, whether she had sought some medical advice.

9. Being able to stay with silences and be comfortable with them can be very difficult for some people. But in therapy, silences are often very important. Clients need the space and time to feel things and let them develop. This therapist jumps in with a question, but the client has already said how hard it is to talk about what he feels.

Clients often work very hard during silences. They will share their feelings with you when they are ready to, and when you have shown yourself to be trustworthy.

10. Therapy being what it is, clients often need to express very strongly felt emotions. These might be, for example, despair, feeling suicidal, feeling violently angry or feeling great love and affection. Whatever they are, it is essential that therapists are not afraid of emotions, can be comfortable with their expression, and not feel the need to dampen them down. If clients can't express deep emotion with their therapist, who can they express them with? This therapist appears to be afraid of anger and its open expression.

11. One of the commonest mistakes we see with therapists in training is the way they "latch on" inappropriately to people other than the client. This client's father is not in the room, and it's very doubtful if the client knows how his father feels anyway. Besides, the therapist is there to help the client make sense of *his* world and *his* feelings. Getting the client to talk about someone else in this way is likely to take him away from his present feelings. The therapist should try to stay within the client's frame of reference as much as possible, but in this example, the therapist has diverted attention away from the client's direct experience.

12. This is a home-spun version of Freudianism, which is dangerous because it is the therapist's own theory and shows ignorance and insecurity. It might very well be true that this client has unresolved feelings about her violent father, but is it helpful to point this out in this way? We think probably not. Much better would be to stay with this client and her feelings, and help her explore her past feelings when she is ready to do so, and in her own way.

In general:

Most of the above are examples of therapists trying too hard to "do therapy", rather than form warm, understanding relationships with their clients. In Person-Centred terms, therapy is not something that one person does to another. Change happens when two people experience a relationship that is understanding, non-judgemental and authentic *in the way that Rogers defined and understood those terms*. We can't emphasise too strongly that the relationship has to meet these criteria, otherwise anyone can argue that their relationships with clients are understanding, non-judgemental and authentic.

In Person-Centred therapy, clients are offered relationships which they discover, gradually, to be trustworthy, where their innermost feelings can be expressed without fear, and where they are respected and valued as people in a process of change. This is why the basic attitudes and values of the therapist are so important. Technique cannot hide a lack of understanding, or a judgemental attitude, neither can it make up for a therapist who hides behind a role or facade and is unable to meet clients person to person.

CHECKLIST 6 : THERAPIST ATTITUDES

Carl Rogers offered a series of questions he asked himself about his ability to form creative therapeutic relationships with his clients. We give an abbreviated form here - it is useful as a kind of checklist that can certainly be used in training, but ought to be returned to periodically throughout one's professional life. Before you read through these ideas, take some time now to stop and think through what kinds of questions you have about yourself and your abilities to form good relationships with others. Then compare your questions with the ones offered by Carl Rogers :

1. Can I be, in some way which will be perceived by the other person as trustworthy, as dependable or consistent in some deep sense?

2. Can I be expressive enough as a person to communicate unambiguously what I am?

3. Can I let myself experience positive attitudes towards this other person - attitudes of warmth, caring, liking, interest, respect?

4. Can I be strong enough as a person to be separate from the other? Can I be a sturdy respecter of my own feelings, my own needs as well as his?

5. Am I secure enough within myself to permit him his separateness? Can I permit him to be what he is - honest or deceitful, infantile or adult, despairing or over-confident? Can I give him the freedom to be? Or do I feel that he should follow my advice, or remain somewhat dependent on me, or mould himself after me?

6. Can I let myself enter fully into the world of his feelings and personal meaning and see these as he does? Can I step into his private world so completely that I lose all desire to evaluate or judge it?

7. Can I receive him as he is? Can I communicate this attitude? Or can I only receive him conditionally, acceptant of some aspects of his feelings and silently or openly disapproving of other aspects?

8. Can I act with sufficient sensitivity in the relationship for my behaviour not to be perceived as a threat?

9. Can I free him from the threat of external evaluation? In almost every phase of our lives - at home, at school, at work - we find ourselves under the rewards and punishments of external judgements.

10. Can I meet this person as a person who is in the process of *becoming* or will I not be open enough to the many possibilities for change both in him and in myself?

Before going on, read through the following checklist which sums up some of the main points we made in this chapter.

CHECKLIST 7: A PHILOSOPHY OF THERAPY

The Person-Centred Approach to counselling and therapy is built on the philosophical assumptions that:

1. People make sense of the world from their own experiences of it, each in their own idiosyncratic ways.

2. People have an inherent capacity to grow, develop and change.

3. The actualising tendency is the only motivational force behind human behaviour.

4. People develop conditions of worth through their interactions with their environment.

5. Therapy aims at full congruence and actualisation of the true self (the organismic self).

6. Therapy helps people to trust their own feelings and experience.

7. A therapeutic relationship of definable qualities provides the context within which change and development can happen.

8. Therapists should try to stay within the client's frame of reference.

CHAPTER FIVE

THE FULLY FUNCTIONING PERSON

The "fully functioning person" as described by Carl Rogers, is an ideal derived from the culture and times when Rogers and his colleagues were working. This cultural context reveals values that are essentially Western, white, middle class and relatively individualistic.

In different cultural settings, and at different times, some of the following characteristics of the fully functioning person might be seen as irrelevant at best, or actually anti-social at worst. The most unhelpful thing would be to regard Rogers' ideas as fixed, or that they claim to be appropriate to all cultures, or that they describe a universal ideal type.

For example, some cultures do not value the individual as highly or in the same way as does Western culture in general. In such cultures, a more appropriate characteristic of the fully functioning person might be the ability to value the welfare and continued survival of the group more highly than valuing oneself.

However, Rogers did offer a general set of values and ways of being which he saw as both enabling individual expression, and valuing social organisation and co-operation. He believed that people were always in the process of "becoming"; they are not entirely rigid or fixed at some stage of development from which it is impossible to develop and move beyond.

Becoming more fully functioning involves a process of becoming more congruent, and more aware of ourselves in relation to others and the environment in which we live. This includes becoming more trusting of experience and feelings, and less reliant on the judgement of others. In technical terms this is referred to as a shift in the *locus of evaluation* from the external (the evaluations of others), to the internal (self-evaluation).

It is possible to observe or determine whether or not a person is becoming more fully functioning; certain characteristics can be observed and described as indicators of this process. In other words, their presence tends to show that a person is developing and growing, and their absence tends to show that a person has become "stuck", though the experience of being stuck need not be a permanent one.

The characteristics described next tend to exist in people with a high degree of personal congruence, but they are not comprehensive, and they are not intended as a kind of diagnosis of what is wrong with us. We might experience these things as being true of us, but not all the time and not in every circumstance. Change is often a very fluid process; at times we move towards being more fully functioning, and at others we move away from it. Psychotherapy often tends to be like this, with two steps forward and one step back, but over time the general direction will be a movement towards positive outcomes, with some gains being made more easily than others.

EXERCISE 24: Your ideas about the fully functioning person

Aims of the exercise
To explore ideas about what constitutes a fully functioning person.

What to do
Before you read through the rest of this chapter, stop for a moment, and take some time to think about what you consider to be the fully functioning person. You can do this on your own, but another way is to brainstorm some ideas in a small group.

Think of people you know or have known who seem to you to use more of their personal resources (and have more of them) than most other people. They don't have to be successful people in the conventional sense of being in important or influential positions, though this may also be true of many of the people you can think of.

Make a list of what you come up with, and compare it with the characteristics of the fully functioning person described here.

1. Belief in our own identity

Fully functioning people are able to recognise their *introjected values* (those they have adopted from outside of themselves), and their conditions of worth, and are able to develop values that are more consistent with their basic organismic valuing system.

They are, therefore, fairly secure in who they are and are not confused about their identity. They are clear that they have a rightful place in the world, are able to recognise their needs, and find ways of meeting them.

Confusion about identity involves self-doubt and making negative self judgements which consume internal energy and attention. Spending time worrying and wondering who you are is a very exhausting business. Release from using energy in this way means it can be used more constructively in other directions.

2. Living more fully in the present

Fully functioning people are not trapped in the past, nor are they fearful of the future. This means that more energy and attention is available for the present moment, and they can be more fully engaged in what is happening right now.

Unresolved issues from the past can lead to self-doubt, confusion and repression of feelings. A common experience is for people to know that there is something inside, from the past, that still controls them. They often know it has to be dealt with somehow, but they are either too afraid to, or don't know how.

If we go back for a moment to Jack, our client at the beginning of this book, we notice he says:

Jack: *When I think about that, about what I just said, it does feel like there's another person in me, or perhaps it's another bit of me... who has kept quiet for a* *long time, and not really been happy with what's going on. I mean, the main bit of me is successful and all that, but .... I need to think about this more...*

Here, Jack begins to realise that there is something from the past, some part of his development that got left behind or interrupted in some way. Because of this, he feels some fear about what the future might contain for him :

Jack: *It seems weird, but it does feel a bit like that. Like someone got left behind in the rush to get on with things. But now it's beginning to feel like that part is saying, "what about me?" That scares me a bit, that thought....*

In common with many of us, Jack feels that he has had to pretend to himself that he is OK. This means that life, at least in part, has an unreal quality to it. Jack finds it increasingly difficult to acknowledge his feelings to himself, or express them openly to others.

The process of becoming fully functioning includes being increasingly in touch with feelings, and an increasing trust in them as useful guides to our values and behaviour. Because we are not so afraid of feelings, we have less need to deny them, and this means that more of our attention is available for living in the present moment.

3. Valuing all of oneself

Our culture tends to encourage us to think of ourselves as divided into different aspects, as if they are only vaguely connected to each other. For example, we think of the intellectual, the physical, emotional and spiritual as distinctly different, almost independent aspects of ourselves.

Becoming more fully functioning includes an integration of these aspects into a unified whole, so that none need to be expressed at the expense of others, and all are available to be expressed equally according to our needs.

Many times people are uneasy with the emotional part of themselves, particularly emotions that are negatively valued such as fear and anger. They may also be afraid to acknowledge and express feelings of love, or tenderness. They feel that such emotions are in control of them, or could take them over in some way, and they want to be in control of their feelings. Our ideal, fully functioning person is aware that emotions are present for good and valid reasons, and that they play an important part in life. Emotions are indications that something either positive or negative (or sometimes a mixture of these) is taking place. If they are acknowledged and valued they can help us move on. Of course the acknowledgement of some feelings can itself be a painful process.

Recognition of the important role of emotions in our functioning often has a releasing effect on other aspects of human experience, and enhances the quality of living. This is especially true for those of us who were taught to squash feelings, or mistrust them in some way.

4. Experiencing life as a process

Openness to experience, and a willingness to accept responsibility for their role in that experience, are strong characteristics of fully functioning people. They have discovered that trusting in themselves and acting on that trust brings positive benefits.

Fully functioning people are just as able to suffer hurt and pain as anyone else, but they have the resources to deal more effectively with them. They are also able fully to experience, appreciate and enjoy the more positive aspects of life.

None of us knows what the future holds, but if we can act on our own basic beliefs, then the consequences of our actions can be integrated into our own developing meaning systems; we can learn something definite from our experiences. If we act on how we believe we *ought* to act, determined by the pressures of others, then it is more difficult to develop our own points of view, or to grow, because it is more difficult to integrate our experiences.

Fully functioning people tend not to have fixed goals or endpoints for themselves or their relationships, and often they are sceptical of conventional measures of success. A basic trust in themselves, and a strong desire to have meaningful, purposeful and authentic lives are much more important.

5. Purpose and meaning in life

Fully functioning people tend to have a high level of self-esteem; they see themselves as people of high value as human beings, but not in a competitive sense or at the expense of others. As social beings, they like to make contributions to the benefit of society as a whole, and because of their strong belief in themselves, they are not dependent on others for approval of their contributions.

They can integrate with, or adapt to society in a balanced way, recognising society's values for what they are, and preserving the integrity of their own value systems.

6. Healthy scepticism of society

Fully functioning people have a strong desire for authenticity; they would like to see it in society as well as in themselves. They tend to reject anything that indicates hypocrisy, deceit, secrecy and double standards.

They are, for example, suspicious of the dominant values and philosophies of science and technology. This does not mean that they are against scientific advances, but want to see them used to enhance the quality of life for everyone on the planet, and not in ways that destroy people or threaten the environment.

They tend to avoid bureaucratic institutions that can de-personalise human beings, and they do not like to give up their power to experts, officials and professionals.

7. Interpersonal relationships

Fully functioning people are aware of the need for their total "humanness" to be given attention and to find expression. They value authenticity in relationships and avoid game playing.

For fully functioning people, deep trusting relationships in which they can be themselves without barriers to communication, are very important. They have developed the ability to maintain their own uniqueness and identity while being absorbed in relationships with others.

In all relationships, fully functioning people are concerned with the nurturing aspects of relationships, they enjoy intimacy and are able to be vulnerable without fear.

They value open communication with others with whom they feel close, and they can give non-possessive love and caring as well as receive it.

8. Creativity

Fully functioning people enjoy high levels of personal creativity. This does not necessarily mean in the conventional sense of art, music or literature, but in all aspects of their lives. They are willing to take risks, and to find new and creative "ways of being", which they can bring to their personal and professional relationships.

They tend to be innovative and experimental, and are often at the forefront of change. They see change as both necessary and desirable, and are interested in new ideas, especially those that are concerned with quality in life.

Growing towards fully functioning

As we said at the beginning of this chapter, the concept of the fully functioning person is that of an ideal towards which it is possible to grow, rather than something which *must* be achieved. If you did the exercise at the beginning of this chapter, you will have your own ideas about what constitutes such a person, and you may disagree with some of the comments above, or want to add to them. The important thing is to recognise that people do make changes that have meaning and value for them. In psychotherapy, people tend to make choices to change in directions that are social and creative, rather than anti-social or destructive of themselves or others.

It is the actualising tendency that provides the "energy" for positive, creative changes to happen. Carl Rogers believed that growth, change and development towards full actualisation are natural for all organisms, and saw no reason why human beings should be excluded from this process.

Growing towards greater congruence, and becoming more fully functioning are the general goals of therapy, but how clients achieve these things will naturally vary from one person to another.

Yet even though everybody is different, we can see a similar process taking place each time. This does not mean that therapy is totally predictable, or that the process is a smooth one, but there does seem to be a series of stages through which clients travel on their journey towards becoming more fully functioning, more of who they are.

Rogers thought that there were seven of these stages that he could observe, and they enabled him to see whether his clients were making progress in therapy, or whether they seemed to be stuck, for a time unable to move on. Although the process can be erratic, clients do, in general, progress step by step, building on their experiences at one stage before moving on to the next. Only when people feel accepted and understood at one stage, do they feel able to take the next step.

This *process scale* is quite complex, but here we give a simplified version to show the basic characteristics of each of the seven stages.

Stage 1

People in this stage appear to be rigid in personality and rather remote, cut off from their emotions and from other people. Rogers thought it unlikely that such people would see any value in therapy, and therefore unlikely that they would take part in it.

People in stage one are very unwilling to reveal anything about themselves, especially their feelings, with which they are very unfamiliar anyway. They tend to see things in terms of opposites - good or bad, right or wrong, with very little in between. They are governed by rigid rules as to how people should behave, and they are strongly judgemental of others, having a rather pessimistic view of human nature. They tend to cope with life in ways that divert attention away from themselves and their feelings, and they view a display of emotion as a weakness. Typical of this stage are statements like:

> "Talking about feelings is a waste of time."

> "Students are all the same."

> "People ought to do as they are told."

These kinds of generalised statements indicate a very rigid view of the world where everything has its place, and ambiguity and uncertainty are very difficult to tolerate. The world is seen as an unfriendly, even hostile place, and that is how it is and how it will stay.

Stage 2

Here, there is a slight loosening of rigid constructs, though people find it very difficult to accept any responsibility for themselves, or what happens in their lives. When things go wrong, they tend to blame others, and feel like victims of a hostile world, rather than participators in it.

"I'm not responsible when things go wrong, am I?"

"I don't do anything wrong, other people keep creating problems for me."

"No-one ever sees my good side, they only ever see the bad."

There is more of an acceptance that things are not right in their lives, but any fault tends to lie in others, or the world in general.

Stage 3

The loosening of attitudes continues as people are more willing to talk about themselves though they tend to do so in the third person, particularly when it's about feelings:

"This is how you feel when someone does something like this to you, isn't it."

"After all, people do have feelings."

People are less comfortable expressing presently experienced feelings, and more comfortable talking about feelings that happened in the past:

"When I was a kid, I did a lot of things that made me feel bad. I just couldn't tell anyone about them because of what would have happened if I did". Internal contradictions start to emerge, and the differences between an idealised self and the reality of the situation start to become apparent:

"I try so hard to be the perfect husband, but it just doesn't work out. I fail all the time."

"I feel I'd like to really achieve something in life, but I never get round to doing anything about it."

"I don't know why I never succeed at the things I try. Maybe that's the way I am. I'm just doomed to failure."

In this stage there may be hints that there are different possibilities available, but there is still a tendency to see things in hard and fast terms - if they're not one thing, then they must be the opposite. If not good, then bad; if not a success, then a failure.

Clients who first seek therapy are often at this stage and need to be fully accepted as they present themselves before moving deeper into stage four.

Stage 4

In this stage, clients begin to describe deeper feelings, usually those that happened in the past.

> "I felt so desperately unhappy when she didn't seem to care. I've never known such deep feelings, it really scared me."

People have difficulty in understanding and accepting these (negative) feelings and would rather they hadn't existed.

> "If this is what falling in love means, then I'd rather not have it."

Feelings in the present start to emerge, but they are mistrusted and even rejected.

> "There's this knot, deep down inside, which stops me from doing things and being myself. I don't know what it is, and that makes me angry. What can I do about it?"

Notice that the client is starting to accept responsibility for what is happening, even though the fearfulness and hopelessness of it are apparent.

There may be some recognition of patterns that occur in the experience of life, sometimes accompanied by a wry humour.

> "It's crazy, isn't it, the way I keep setting myself up for the same old let down. Look at me, a man of forty, acting like a kid."

Also at this stage, clients begin to enter into more direct relationships with their therapist, but there is often a fearfulness about this.

> "I find it difficult to trust people, I even find myself wondering how much I can trust you."

Explorations of this kind are common in therapy and the loosening up of expression continues into the next stages. These later stages are quite complex, and result in many different ways of expression and viewing of the world.

Stage 5

Clients are never wholly at one stage of the process or another. They may start to move on, then take a step back, rather like dipping a toe into the water and deciding it's too cold (or too hot), to go for a swim.

It is when people feel fully accepted and understood that they feel free to explore deeper feelings. The therapist's role is not to lead them from one stage to the next, but to provide them with opportunities to experience fully each stage in their own process, and in their own unique ways.

By stage five, clients feel more confident about expressing presently experienced feelings:

"I experience a lot of rejection in my life, and I wonder - is that how it's going to be with you too, will you end up rejecting me? At the moment I feel quite afraid of this."

The developing freedom and ability to express current feelings means that they are less likely to be denied. They can start to bubble up inside, and even though they are not fully understood or wholly accepted, clients can find ways of expressing them, however tentatively.

"I've just realised something. When I start feeling unsure of myself, I get this strange feeling inside which sort of strangles me, and stops me from being all of myself. It is happening now, but it's gradually fading."

There can be a feeling of getting close to something important, but not being able to get into direct contact with it. There is still a reluctance to trust feelings in themselves, they can be talked about but not fully experienced.

New insights about life and relationships also start to emerge.

" I thought I was bad because I felt angry at my father. Now I realise that I was angry because I was hurt. It's obvious to me now that if I get hurt, it's natural to get angry. It all makes sense now. It doesn't mean that I have to feel love for him all the time, he's not perfect, and neither am I."

Here, the client is acknowledging and accepting ambivalent feelings towards another person, and that it is OK to have these contradictory feelings alongside each other.

Stage 6

Rogers described this stage as being very distinctive and often dramatic. It is characterised by feelings, previously suppressed, becoming fully experienced in the present moment. This awareness is acute, clear and full of meaning. The self which hitherto has been experienced as somewhat fragmented is now experienced as an integrated whole - mind, body, emotion and intellect, and clients experience moments of full congruence.

Previously felt ambiguities and uncertainties now start to click into place and become crystal clear. These experiences are irreversible and produce changes in attitude and perception that are quite remarkable. The way the world is viewed is never the same again.

Feelings start to flow freely and reach their full conclusion. Previous fears about the potential destructiveness of negative feelings evaporate, and feelings are seen as enriching experiences, not ones to be avoided.

One of the most striking discoveries made by many people at this stage is the realisation of care, concern and tenderness for oneself.

"You know, when I look back and see myself as a three year old, and looking at what I had to put up with, I really do feel sorry for myself. And now, when I look at myself, I feel tender and loving towards myself. I know that I need to take care of me, and treat myself kindly and well....I never knew it was possible to feel this way...it feels really good... really warm".

Carl Rogers uses the following example in his book, *On Becoming a Person*:

The client, a young man, has expressed the wish that his parents would die or disappear.

88

Client: *It's kind of like wanting to wish them away, and wishing they had never been...And I'm so ashamed of myself because then they call me, and off I go - swish! They're somehow still so strong. I don't know. There's some umbilical - I can almost feel it inside me - swish* (and he gestures, plucking himself away by grasping at his navel.)

Therapist: *They really do have a hold on your umbilical cord.*

Client: *It's funny how real it feels ... like a burning sensation, kind of, and when they say something which makes me anxious I can feel it right here* (pointing). *I never thought of it quite that way.*

Therapist: *As though if there's a disturbance in the relationship between you, then you do feel it as though it was a strain on your umbilicus.*

Client: *Yeah, kind of like in my gut here. It's so hard to define the feeling that I feel there.*

Rogers says, of this example: "Here he is living subjectively in the feeling of dependence on his parents. Yet it would be most inaccurate to say that he is perceiving it. He is *in* it, experiencing it as a strain on his umbilical cord. In *this* stage, internal communication is free and relatively unblocked."

Rogers also comments: "And, it might be remarked in passing, once an experience is fully in awareness, fully accepted, then it can be coped with effectively, like any other clear reality."

Stage 7

Rogers thought that changes made by clients in stage six tended to be irreversible, and further change was as likely to occur outside of the therapeutic relationship as within it. By this stage people are effecting change for themselves, and the need for therapy is more or less over.

In the therapeutic situation itself, client and therapist are actively collaborating to explore ways in which new-found confidence can be used and expressed in the world outside. Clients are open to experience, are able to trust their own feelings, and have developed a strong internal locus of evaluation.

There is a fluid, changing quality to life, as people are able to experience each new event without being bound by interpretations that belong in the past. There is a strong feeling of living fully in the present, an ability to relate freely to others, and an awareness that further change and growth is not only possible, but desirable.

Very few people enter therapy at a particular stage and go on through to stage seven. Many leave therapy at an earlier point, and if therapy has been successful for them, content that real and meaningful change has happened.

Remember that this *Process Scale* represents an idealised view of the therapeutic process, it indicates the flow of events in a very general way. Each person will experience therapy differently, will have different concerns, and will be content to leave therapy at different points. It is useful as a way of thinking about the process that we go through on the journey towards becoming fully-functioning, it isn't a prescription of what we must do in order to get there.

Moments of movement

The normal experience for clients in making progress through the stages we have previously described, is that rarely (if ever) is there a smooth transition from one stage to the next. There are often periods of time in which little progress can be observed or felt, and then something happens that moves the process on a little.

Carl Rogers thought that there were times in therapy during which people took a definite step forward, and he described them as *moments of movement.*

A moment of movement occurs when people have a direct experience of some aspect of themselves without inhibition, that up till that moment had been denied or distorted in some way. This is the first time this experience has been allowed fully into awareness, and it is accompanied by the realisation that it is an acceptable part of the person, not one of which to be ashamed. An example of this, which is taken from a paper Rogers gave to the first meeting of the American Academy of Psychotherapists in 1956, will help to make it clearer :

Client: *It's just being terribly hurt!. . . And then, of course, I've come to see and to feel that over this. . . see, I've covered it up.*

A moment later she puts it slightly differently.

Client: *You know, it's almost a physical thing. It's... sort of as though I were looking within myself at all kinds of... nerve endings and - bits of... things that have been sort of mashed* (weeping).

Therapist: *As though some of the most delicate aspects of you - physically almost - have been crushed or hurt.*

Client: *Yes. And you know, I do get the feeling, oh, you poor thing.*

Therapist: *You just can't help but feel very deeply sorry for the person that is you.*

This experience has the quality of being immediate - it occurs now, and is not a thought or an intellectual insight. Although much of it may have been experienced in different ways before, never so completely, and never with the awareness of it accompanied by such intense physiological reactions. It is accepted as part of the self, and not disowned or denied. Personal integration and congruence are general goals of therapy and this is an example of what integration and congruence mean. The person's feelings flow freely, are accepted and expressed directly.

Rogers suggested that therapy can be described as being made up of moments such as this, in which an increasing number of experiences previously denied or covered up, are experienced directly and integrated into the person's sense of self. The content of these moments varies from one person to the next, the main characteristic is that up until this point it has been thought of as unacceptable to the person involved.

Person-Centred therapy is not a mechanical process, in which each step follows smoothly from the one before, but there are general characteristics of the process that are recognisable, and so to this extent predictable. Rogers was concerned to discover ways that the inner, personal power of the client could be mobilised to enable movement towards full congruence.

In a later chapter, we look at ways in which Person-Centred therapy is similar to many other kinds of therapy, but Person-Centred therapy is unique in that it sees the formation of a special kind of relationship as the prime means by which positive change is initiated. This approach to therapy brings with it some risks, as well as possibilities for profound personal change. We leave this chapter with Rogers' own words :

" I enter the relationship not as a scientist, not as a physician who can accurately diagnose and cure, but as a person entering into a personal relationship. Insofar as I see him only as an object, the client will tend to become only an object. I risk myself, because if, as the relationship deepens, what develops is a failure, a regression, a repudiation of me and the relationship by the client, then I . . . will lose . . . a part of myself" (*On Becoming a Person*).

CHAPTER SIX

ENCOUNTER GROUPS

What is an Encounter Group?

Encounter Groups are places where people can spend some time together exploring their relationships with each other, and sharing in each person's life experience. They can be places which help people focus on those aspects of life that are the cause of some concern for them, and they afford opportunities for meeting others and getting to know them in an atmosphere of trust and understanding. They provide opportunities to develop greater personal congruence, and to receive feedback on changes in our behaviour and attitudes.

The "leader" of an Encounter Group is called the *facilitator*, and the facilitator's job in a group is very similar to the therapist's role with a single client. In some kinds of Encounter Group, the facilitator plays a very active role, suggesting games and exercises that participants can try to help them focus on particular issues, but Person-Centred group facilitators tend to take a more back seat role, and are concerned mostly with ensuring that all participants are fully heard.

The distinction between an Encounter Group and a therapy group is not always easy to make. In therapy groups, activity tends to focus on individual participants one at a time, with the facilitator or another group member giving intensive attention - like conducting individual therapy in a group setting. Although this may happen sometimes in an Encounter Group, the emphasis tends to be more on the relationships among group members, and ways in which they may help each other. Therapy groups often contain people who are experiencing quite serious personal problems, whilst Encounter Groups tend to be more for people who are functioning reasonably well, but looking to enrich their personal development and discover more authentic ways of relating to others.

These days, Encounter Groups are not as popular as they once were. At one time, Encounter Groups were widely available, and offered as one-off events by just about every school of therapy and personal growth around. Many times these groups took place over a weekend in a residential setting, or were offered as a series of meetings over a number of evenings.

Encounter Groups have ranged in style, goals and methods from small, intimate groups to huge ones of over two hundred people. In the nineteen sixties and seventies it was being claimed that people's lives could be transformed through participation in one or more of these groups. Group Encounter went through a period of bad press with people being accused of using such groups to encourage bizarre sexual practices, or to brainwash people into joining peculiar quasi-religious sects, and so on. It is certainly true that in the early days some groups were badly led by inexperienced facilitators, but stories of people being seriously damaged by their experiences in groups always turned out to be highly exaggerated. Encounter Groups were seized on by many as the answer to alienation, loneliness and depression, but the truth of the matter is probably far more sober. Groups can be places for profound personal change, they can help people learn to relate to others better, and they can be part of a more general process of growth and development.

It is our experience that Encounter Groups are used quite widely in the training of therapists and counsellors, and this seems especially true for Person-Centred therapists.

The Basic Encounter Group

Carl Rogers was one of a number of people who developed the idea of the Encounter Group, and he called his approach the *Basic Encounter Group*. In these groups the same values and attitudes apply as with individual therapy -

that people can be trusted to find ways of relating that are creative and meaningful for them, provided that an atmosphere of empathy, congruence and positive regard can be developed. The facilitator's role is to help establish this climate, and the best way of doing this is to offer group members empathic understanding, genuineness and non-judgemental care, rather than talk about these conditions.

In the Basic Encounter Group, facilitators are generally content to follow the group in whatever direction it chooses to take - they do not have set agendas for such groups. This means paying attention to and respecting all expression and communication, whether so-called negative or positive feelings are being expressed.

This does not mean, however, that facilitators are passive, any more than the individual therapist is passive. The word "facilitate" means "to make easier", but it doesn't mean "to direct" or "control".

Facilitators can provide something of a model for group members in their way of being, not so that members can copy what they do, but to encourage them to find ways of being more understanding of others and genuine in their relationships. Perhaps one important role is to ensure that groups do not scapegoat individuals, or become oppressive towards some members.

The question of power

It is inescapable that in many ways, group facilitators have more power than ordinary group members, or at least are perceived as having more power. The facilitator may be the most experienced person in groups in the room, will probably have been designated as facilitator in advance of the group meeting, and so on. How facilitators deal with issues of power will depend on how well they have internalised a set of attitudes and values that are empowering of others, and not manipulative of them. The same, of course, is true of the individual therapist.

Because the Basic Encounter Group does not rely on techniques, games or exercises which may, in themselves, have manipulative qualities, the issue of power is a not as critical as it can be in groups which rely on charismatic leaders, suggestion, persuasion or some other form of confrontation, but this does not dispense with the issue of power completely.

What happens in Encounter Groups?

Encounter Groups are really places for sharing the problems and successes of life, with people who value open communication and active listening. For people who, in their daily lives, are compelled to play some kind of role or to hide their true feelings, they can be places to experience themselves as the people they really feel themselves to be.

Basic Encounter Groups tend to consist mainly of verbal communication, and people usually sit round in a circle on chairs, or cushions if they feel more comfortable that way. Other styles of Encounter include more body work where people move around a lot more, but this is generally not our experience of Basic Encounter, though it certainly is not excluded if this is what participants want.

Encounter Groups are places where feelings and emotions are likely to be expressed. It is possible (and it often happens) for people to use Encounter Groups to help rid themselves of destructive or self-defeating behaviours, and this can be accompanied by very deeply expressed feelings. At such times, people can begin to feel quite vulnerable and afraid, and here the skills and sensitivity of the facilitator become very important.

Just as in individual therapy, the facilitator tries to ensure that people are heard and understood in an atmosphere free of judgement. In this atmosphere, defensive barriers tend to dissolve and more authentic person-to-person encounters become possible. The experience of emerging from behind defensive walls and meeting people more openly can be transferred into daily life, and it is this aspect that many people find most helpful about Encounter Groups. In other words, they can experience what it is like to be more congruent in a safe atmosphere - a kind of dress rehearsal.

Stages of group development

People don't start to relate to each other openly at the drop of a hat, just because they are now in an Encounter Group. People need time to explore how safe this environment really is before they take risks with it. There does seem to be a series of stages through which groups develop on their way to becoming safe places where open communication happens more easily. Carl Rogers described six stages of development of Encounter Groups which we can summarise briefly:

1. Communication is about things external to the group. There is an unwillingness to communicate self. Close relationships are seen as dangerous.

2. People are remote from their subjective experience and feelings remain unowned and external. Expression is about non-self topics. There may be some recognition of inner conflict, but it is seen as external to the self.

3. Feelings which are not actually present in the "here and now" are described, and are often characterised as unacceptable. There may be some communication about the self, but as a reflected object existing primarily in others. There is the beginning of a recognition that problems exist inside the person rather than externally to him or her.

4. Intense feelings are described as not now present. There is a recognition that denied feelings may break through into the present, and this is an unwelcome possibility. Expression of self-responsibility for problems increases. There is an occasional willingness to relate to others in the group on a feeling basis.

5. Feelings are fully expressed as they are experienced in the present and are owned and accepted. Previously denied feelings begin to "bubble through" into awareness. There is an expressed desire to be "the real me", and the person has a definite feeling of responsibility for problems and conflicts existing within him or her.

6. Immediate feelings are no longer denied, feared or struggled against. This experiencing is often a dramatic release for the individual. There is a complete acceptance that feelings provide usable referents for gaining insight into the

meanings of the individual's life. The individual risks him or herself in relating directly to others.

It is no coincidence that these six stages are similar to the stages in individual therapy discussed in an earlier chapter in this book. The Encounter Group is approached with the same level of trust in people's capacities to become less defensive, more congruent and more acceptant of others, as are clients in individual therapy. The roles of facilitator and therapist are very similar and this is a reflection of the basic trust that the actualising tendency can operate on a group and even social level as well as on the individual level.

The extra dimension that Encounter Groups offer is that a group enables personal explorations to be made in the company of others. Groups have a richness and diversity of experience available that provides opportunities for people to enter into a variety of different relationships.

Encounter in therapist training.
Most training programmes in Person-Centred counselling of which we know include some element of Group Encounter. In a training context, Encounter Groups enable would-be therapists to experience directly what it can be like to take risks, to open up and trust others, and to hear and empathise with a lot of different people. The possibilities of receiving feedback from other members of the group enable us to check on how well we express ourselves, how empathic we are being, how much judgementalism we show and how congruent we are felt to be.

This last point is one of the most useful ways of using an Encounter Group in therapist training - to provide a situation where people can learn to become more congruent. Struggling to form more authentic relationships with other members of the group provides good learning that can be used in individual therapy. Where, for example, two people are attempting to communicate but failing to understand each other, other group members can facilitate the dialogue by summarising, rephrasing and reflecting. The wisdom of the group can be a powerful force in helping to clarify misunderstandings, and encouraging people to communicate more directly, and with increasing sensitivity towards others.

CHAPTER SEVEN

ON BEING A CLIENT....

Learning to become more empathic, more congruent and less judgemental through training and exercises is one thing, actually experiencing these attitudes for yourself is something else.

We said earlier that one of the best ways of learning to be more empathic is to have experiences of being deeply understood oneself. Somehow, these experiences teach us about the value of good listening; it becomes meaningful in an emotional sense, not just in an intellectual one.

Being in the receiving role, either as a client in individual therapy, or as a member of an Encounter Group (preferably both) is a very important, perhaps essential, preparation for any would-be therapist. Apart from just experiencing and learning to appreciate good Person-Centred therapist attitudes and ways of being, getting your own therapy helps to free you from self-defeating behaviour or attitudes, allows you to explore your own psychological history, and helps you to become clearer and more congruent.

Subsequent relationships with clients are then less likely to be confused by therapists inadvertently working on their own unconscious needs. Also, if therapy has worked for you, you are much more likely to trust the process of therapy, and much more able to stay with clients through the difficult times.

Next, we give two brief examples of how we experienced therapy as clients. The first one tells of something that happened during an Encounter Group, and the second is of how it felt to be in individual therapy.

1. Tony Merry

I have chosen this particular incident from among many for a number of reasons. Firstly, I like it very much and it came at an important time for me. It concerns my experiences of being a father and led to some very deep explorations of my own childhood, so this story is only the beginning of a much longer process. Secondly, the group was being facilitated by Carl Rogers, and I think this is a good example of the way he tended to work in groups - staying in the background, but listening carefully and speaking when he was moved to do so. Thirdly, the other group members were very important to me (some still are), and I enjoy recalling some of the times we spent together.

The theme of this group at the time this incident took place was whether or not the whole therapy/personal growth idea was really doing anyone any good in a world beset with political and social problems. Wasn't it all a bit of an indulgence?

I began to talk about how I felt my attitudes and values were beginning to change, how I felt Person-Centred ideas to be making a real difference to me, and how I was beginning to see myself making real changes that involved more people than just me. I told the group this short story about my daughter Kate, who had just started playschool.

It seemed that Kate had experienced some trouble at playschool one morning. She was doing some colouring-in when the child next to her snatched away the crayons because she wanted to use them too. This put Kate into something of a dilemma. She wanted to finish her picture, and she was willing to share the crayons, but she certainly wasn't prepared to have them snatched away like this. The situation was never satisfactorily resolved. The play leader simply took the crayons away, and the incident finished with tears all round, with Kate feeling frustrated and that what had happened simply wasn't fair.

I told my group how I had really listened to this story from Kate. I could hear the anger and frustration in her voice, her desire to be fair, and how she felt let down by the play leader. I don't remember the exact words I said to Kate, but they added up to something like: "Well, I guess that made you really cross, when you tried your hardest to share things and be fair, and it all went wrong. It does feel bad when things don't work out right, even when you try your best, doesn't it?"

I told the group that really listening to Kate, and trying to see the world through the eyes of a young child, helped Kate feel taken seriously and her mixture of feelings acknowledged and understood. Whatever it was I said to her, it obviously hit the nail on the head, because she lit up like a Christmas tree, and told me everything that had happened to her during the whole day, almost without stopping. When she had finished, she gave me a hug and went off to play with her brother.

In the group, I said to no-one in particular: "What I most hope for, if it's at all possible, is to be able to listen to my children the best way I can, to be there for them, and to learn to love them without needing to control them. Perhaps if I can succeed in this, they won't have to spend hours in Encounter Groups when they are thirty-five undoing all the damage their father did to them."

This was partly a joke, and partly serious. I made a joke of it because at that time I was very unsure of myself as a father, and I didn't want to admit to myself how afraid I really was at being responsible for such young children.

Carl said: "It sounds to me as if they have their Encounter Group already."

This simple response, the warmth of which I cannot capture in the written word, was like a breath of fresh air. In a single moment, Carl showed me that he had really listened to what I had said, and understood something that at the time I hardly understood myself. Somehow he had sensed a real struggle going on in me. Supposing it turned out that I really was a no-good father? Supposing I didn't know how to love my children enough? In that moment, I became aware of that internal struggle, even though I had tried to hide it from myself (and others) by making a joke out of it.

This was a very brief moment, but it had a profound effect on me. It led, over the next few weeks, to some very intense exploration of my feelings about being a father, and it helped me gain some insights into my own early childhood. It started off a process that was a very significant one in my life. In some ways it is still going on. I feel it made me more understanding of my own parenting, and I became more at ease and confident with my children.

It seems to me that this is often how Person-Centred therapy works. There are periods of time in which important insights like this happen. They start off a process which goes deeper and deeper, until there is a kind of resolution, when feelings are fully felt in the moment, and you gain some realisation of something that shifts your whole perspective. It isn't talking about an experience, it is actually *having* the experience, or reliving an experience in the immediate moment that is a powerful force for change.

I know that during that group meeting I had a real experience of being a person struggling with something that made me afraid. The matter wasn't resolved there and then, but I felt I had been heard, and, just as importantly, felt that I had listened to myself.

2. Bob Lusty

The act of putting into print some of my experiences as a client in therapy feels somewhat risky, as it is very personal, and leaves me feeling vulnerable. However, I do value the experience, and as I also believe in openness, I offer it to you.

Going to see a therapist was a nerve wracking decision to make. Up until that point, I had led my life thinking that I had to keep my innermost thoughts to myself, particularly those that I felt to be shameful. I thought that if I encountered any significant problems, I ought to be able to sort them out on my own. In fact it was some kind of test that I did do it alone, but I found myself going round and round in circles, and I simply didn't know how to solve things myself. I was well and truly stuck, and in emotional turmoil.

Having made the appointment, I anticipated it with mixed feelings. On the one hand, I didn't look forward to having to reveal myself, that felt very vulnerable, and I was concerned that I would feel judged. On the other hand I expected that whatever happened it would be helpful to me. In order for it to be helpful, I had to be honest - no hiding or game playing.

After an initial introduction, the therapist asked me what I wanted to talk to him about, so it was straight over to me. I found myself sitting opposite a person giving me his full attention with a quiet intensity. It was not like a conversation, but more of a dialogue charged with a special quality where there were definite expectations on me as a person. I blurted out my problems, trying to be as accurate as I could. I found the relief of being able to unburden myself quite a tearful experience. My fear of being judged was completely unfounded, and I felt fully accepted and liberated.

As I went on I felt clearly that I had to take responsibility for myself; the therapist didn't show any sign of taking responsibility for me. They were my problems, and I was the only one who could discover the answers. It was also obvious that he wouldn't take any avoidance from me in my confused state, and I felt quite challenged by this.

That first session didn't provide any answers, but I felt I had made a good start. I felt relieved that I had actually begun to confront things, and even though I didn't know where it was going, it felt a positive and powerful experience.

It took me a while to get used to therapy, to learn how to use the time most effectively. Gradually, I discovered I could trust myself more and more, and that I could take responsibility for myself in the therapeutic relationship. I became increasingly aware of my innermost feelings during the therapy sessions themselves, feelings that I usually suppressed in everyday life in case they got too uncomfortable. Through the experience of being fully accepted by my therapist, I was able to communicate what I felt and the vulnerability that went along with my feelings.

Gradually, as I learned to listen to and accept these scary feelings, there came a point when they couldn't be suppressed any longer. Here, it was important that my therapist wasn't afraid of my feelings; he didn't try to interpret them or avoid them in any way. When I could express them I discovered that they were rooted way back in the past, but now I was able to contact them fully in the present. It was as though the past and present had become fused into one. It was an experience that involved the physical, emotional and intellectual sides

103

of me, and a little later, I had an intense spiritual experience which appeared to be a consequence of this greater integration and congruence.

Shortly after this, I decided to stop therapy for a time. I felt much more whole, integrated and confident. I was more aware of myself, and more able to take care of myself. My perception of my life and what had previously been problematic had shifted. My trust in myself and my ability to evaluate what was good or bad for me was much stronger.

My experiences of therapy have been creative and empowering for me. Being a client has helped enormously in my understanding of the process of therapy, and has enabled me to be a much better therapist. I certainly know how it can feel, and how the attitudes of a therapist can affect the client's experience.

....AND ON BEING A THERAPIST

A mixture of thoughts and words come up for us when we try to describe what it is like to be a Person-Centred therapist - exciting, exasperating, frustrating, tender, warm, challenging, creative, difficult, rewarding, and much more.

Next we try to give some insight into the process as we have experienced it. We describe a little of what we try to do, and how we feel when it goes right and when it seems to go wrong. Sometimes the process is so fast it is breathtaking, at other times things slow down, perhaps go round in circles for a while, and then take off in new and unexpected directions.

We don't feel we always succeed, or that we couldn't have done more, been more empathic or more congruent. But there have been times when it has been a profound privilege to have shared in people's lives and growth towards becoming more of who they are.

1. Tony Merry

Once, when I worked in a large "mental hospital" in the south of England as a twenty-year old, I looked around me and wondered how human beings could have ended up in this sorry place. One of the most distressing things was the lack of individual human contact the patients received. They were like cattle, herded from one place to another, hardly ever considered or treated with respect and dignity.

I often wonder if it was this experience, of being surrounded by so many people who had simply been written off, that prompted me to try and make some kind of contribution that would value everyone's individuality, that would look to people's strengths, potential and achievements rather than to their failings. If it was, it lay dormant for a long time, but I believe it had a profound impact on me, and ten years later I took the first steps on the road to responding to that half forgotten experience.

Now, when I see clients for the first time I feel expectant, respectful and wanting to value their dignity, and to discover their uniqueness. First and foremost, I am quite simply, interested. I am curious to meet with them, willing to share part of myself with them and willing to receive from them whatever they are able to offer.

I am often surprised at how inventive and creative people can be. Even when their experiences have been terrible for them, they have discovered some part that has been able to survive, some strength that lies somewhere inside that they have hardly been able to recognise themselves.

I once had a client who I saw almost every week for over a year. She had been abused for many years from the age of about five or six by several male relatives. When she first came to me, she was desperate. She had never been able to have any kind of close relationship with a man, understandably she could not trust any of them. She was now in her middle forties, and had several times been on the edge of suicide. She felt worthless, corrupted, and angry, but most of all guilty.

She had given a relationship one last try, and emerged from it emotionally battered, exhausted and deeply depressed. In our first few meetings, she could hardly bring herself to look at me, and spoke very little. At the end of our third session, I too felt exhausted. I seriously doubted if I had anything I could offer her that she would be able to accept. I spoke with my supervisor for hours, not about her, but about myself as a man confronted by a deeply distrustful woman, and the feelings this aroused in me.

Very gradually she started to talk. She seemed to have made some kind of decision that I was her last chance. In the fifth session she started to tell me her story, slowly and carefully at first, but then faster as if she wanted to get it all out at once. For nearly an hour, I said almost nothing, but I sat with her and I listened. Every now and again she looked quickly up at me to check on my reaction.

When she arrived for the next session she said that she had felt worse than ever for the first two days after we had last met. She had never told anyone a tenth of what she had told me. She couldn't understand why she had said everything the way she did, and she had felt exposed, found out and guilty. But then, in the next few days, things started to change. She felt angry with me for listening to it all, it was as if my hearing what had happened to her somehow implicated me in it. She had felt I was a voyeur, and that I was abusing her too.

I felt shaken. But I understood how telling someone could feel nearly as bad as the thing itself, and that the person you tell almost becomes a part of it. I now knew something about her that nobody else knew, and I guessed that this could make her feel very vulnerable. She started to relax, and she looked at me closely for the first time. She said she had wanted to kill every man she had ever met, and that for a time last week that had included me.

But she came back the next week, and just about every week after that. There were times when I could hardly bear to hear her life story, and there were the times when she could hardly bring herself to tell it. There were times when she cried so hard I thought she might die, and there were times when both of us had tears in our eyes. There were times when we both laughed so much we thought we would burst.

When she decided to stop coming to see me I felt both happy and sad. I had come to know her and, in a way, to love her. During our last session together she said that she wanted me to tell her story to anyone who would listen. Not the details of it, but the fact that she had found a way of learning, really learning, that she was not to blame for what had happened to her, and that this was the most important thing that she had discovered. The last thing she said to me was: "You're not all bad." Recently she wrote to me. She had read an article of mine, and thought she would like to say " Hello". She said she now had two or three close men friends, but that she had decided never again to go into a "complete relationship", and she was happy about that. She said: " I can be a case-study if you like in one of your papers, as long as you don't say my name. I want other women to know that it can be OK if they can find someone who will just listen *and believe them.*"

2. Bob Lusty

The therapeutic relationship is a confidential one in which clients can reveal very important and intimate parts of themselves. They are often very generous in allowing me to share their experiences with others, as in the following examples. I have disguised the identities of the people I am describing, and I try to tell something of their stories with care and respect for them.

Firstly, I feel honoured that someone is prepared to enter into a therapeutic relationship with me. I am clear that I want to provide an environment for them that is as rich as possible in the core conditions.

I try to prepare myself well for each session, giving myself enough time to consider myself and how I am feeling before the session starts. I welcome my clients and try to see that they are comfortable. Directness and respect seem to me to be important ways of showing the value I have for them as human beings.

Clients may begin by talking freely about what is concerning them, sometimes having prepared for the session before it starts. On other occasions I ask how they think I may be able to help, or what they would like to talk about.

I have no preconceived ideas about what the content of each session will be. I am concerned with being available and showing that I am trying to understand as best as I can. This is a very important part of the relationship, when a person feels understood without judgement, distortion or interpretation.

Clients vary as to what they want out of therapy and how they want to use the time. If they see me as a provider of solutions for them, then frustration will arise, and I do my best to acknowledge that frustration. I don't believe I can solve problems for clients, but I do believe that I can help them find their own answers.

I am aware that clients may have sought therapy because they are distressed, confused or in pain to some degree. It feels right to me to acknowledge these realities and not to deny or suppress them. How can confused people be expected to think straight and make clear decisions about themselves? When a person is hurt, I do not want to add to that hurt, so I try to go at the client's pace, carefully and gently. It really is a precious thing for people to trust me with themselves in this way. I have not yet found a situation where I cannot be accepting of another person, even though I may not agree with what they are doing to themselves - when they are abusing drugs dangerously, for example.

I had a client, a young man who was in great difficulty with his parents. A very real problem for him was that he knew himself to be gay, and he wanted to experience gay relationships. He couldn't tell his parents, who he felt would have been shocked and rejecting; they didn't want him to leave home so he felt forced to lie to them about his life, and he became angry with their questions which he felt to be intrusive. He felt that he had to protect his parents from hurt and his family from shame.

Rather than telling him how he could go about leading a more honest life, or what my opinion about the situation was, I said: "It seems you really would like to have a more honest relationship with your parents."

This response, focussing on him and his feelings accurately summed up a good part of how he felt, and he felt very understood by me. It was not for me to approve or disapprove of how he chose to behave in his life, even though I would have preferred him to be happier by being able to live more authentically. We were able to go a long way in exploring how he felt about himself, his life and his relationship with his parents.

On another occasion a client, a woman in her early thirties complained of her depression and frustration at not being able to get on with her college work. It was really important for her to get a qualification, but all her motivation seemed to have disappeared.

As we talked, it started to become clear that her depression and frustration was somehow a symptom of a deep anger. This anger wasn't being expressed directly, but I sensed it in her. Although I wasn't sure, I decided to risk checking out my perception with her, and I said: "It seems as though you're really angry with something or someone, yourself maybe". At this, her eyes lit up. Yes, she was angry.

A few days later she told me how much this session had helped her. Identifying and acknowledging her anger had loosened its hold over her, and she had been able to get down to her studies. It seemed that the energy locked up in the downward spiral of depression and frustration had been released to be used in more creative ways.

I felt a lot of warmth for both this young man and the young woman, and I think this warmth was returned. This feeling is important to me, and it happens all the more when I help create a caring and non-judgemental atmosphere. When clients reveal such feelings I think it is important that I accept them and value them. An expression of feelings of warmth does not mean there is a wish to act on them, and the worst thing I can do is try to deflect them or ignore them. For me it is important that I can accept and understand all of a client's feelings, emotions and expression of feeling. I value all such feelings, whether they are positive or so-called negative. The challenge of therapy for me is to be myself and to enter into relationships with others openly, with care and respect, trusting in them to discover directions for themselves, and trusting in myself to stay with them, however difficult it may sometimes be.

CHAPTER EIGHT

SIMILARITIES AND DIFFERENCES

There is now quite a lot of research to show that psychotherapy, in general, is effective in helping to reduce psychological distress. In one study (by Smith, Glass and Miller, *The Benefits of Psychotherapy*), it was shown that the average person who has received some psychotherapy is better off than 80% of those who had no treatment at all. There is not, however, much research to show that any one specific form of psychotherapy is necessarily any more effective than any other.

This raises an important question - is it the things different psychotherapies have in common that are the effective ingredients, rather than any specific characteristic of particular forms of therapy? One thing that is becoming clearer through research, though, is that the most effective therapists, from whatever orientation, tend to be high in empathic understanding, are seen as "real" people, and are generally non-judgemental.

Next, we explore some of the things that all forms of psychotherapy have in common, and later we discuss how we think Person-Centred therapy is different from other therapies. Though there are many different forms of psychotherapy available (one study by Ivey and Ivey, *Counselling and Psychotherapy: Integrating Skills, Theory and Practice,* described over 250), they can all be grouped under three main headings, though some fit more comfortably than others. They are psychodynamic, behavioural and humanistic/existential. (There are also eclectic forms of therapy which are made up of ideas and methods from a variety of approaches, and which cross the boundaries suggested here).

What makes a form of psychotherapy fit into one or other of these groups includes its goals and methods, but more than anything else its theoretical and philosophical position on questions regarding human nature, the way that personality develops, and the ways in which people are thought to develop psychological disturbance.

You can also distinguish one form of psychotherapy from another by deciding whether it is, for example, oriented towards the gaining of insight into the unconscious, or reliving and re-experiencing incidents and feelings from childhood, or some combination of the two. Some forms of psychotherapy are concerned with re-educating the person away from incorrect or unhelpful concepts of themselves and the world around them, while others concentrate on extinguishing unhealthy behaviours by some kind of systematic learning method. Some focus exclusively on the here and now, while others are more concerned with people's histories and their earliest relationships with parents and other significant people.

Common elements

The most obvious common factor in all forms of psychotherapy is the presence of a client and a therapist. This makes the relationship between these two people, its qualities and the length of time for which it lasts, most significant factors. As we have seen, in Person-Centred therapy it is this relationship that is considered to be the most significant factor. But apart from the qualities of empathy, congruence and positive regard, there are other factors at work too.

The very fact that psychotherapy exists at all is evidence for the widely held belief that people are capable of change - that they are not fixed or conditioned into inflexible or unchangeable ways of being. Clients bring into the therapy room the attitude that change is both within their reach, and something to be desired, even if they do not know what direction those changes may take.

Whatever approach is taken by the therapist, therapy always contains opportunities for clients to disclose and work on their problems. This situation contains a level of trust and respect, in an environment of privacy in which the rules of confidentiality are safeguarded. This makes the therapeutic relationship quite special, different from just about any other kind of relationship. It may (and often does) represent the first time a person has experienced being listened to and taken seriously over an extended period of time.

It may very well be that this aspect of therapy is itself therapeutic. In other words, just being given the opportunity to talk, by someone willing to put his concerns to one side and listen may, on its own, be a powerful and growth-promoting experience. What therapists actually do with what they hear may be of only secondary importance.

Therapy also contains opportunities for clients to re-discover the emotional component of life. This again might be an important factor in itself. Therapy does give people permission to become emotional, and this might be specially important to people who are otherwise denied such opportunities. This has the potential for new personal learning; people can become familiar with and less afraid of their emotional selves, and able to operate in the world with more freedom of expression.

The degree to which different therapies try directly to stimulate emotions varies. Person-Centred therapy does not set out directly to encourage particular feelings (to do this would be to imply that therapy is some "thing" that therapists do to their clients), although some emotional experiencing is inevitable. Other approaches to therapy, though, value the direct stimulation of different emotional states on the grounds that clients expect that therapy will enable them to feel things they haven't felt before, or to come to terms with feelings.

Going to a therapist may legitimise the contacting and expression of feelings in an environment which is accepting and supportive. This again is an experience denied to many people, and the cathartic release of pent-up emotion may be therapeutic of itself.

Another common factor in therapy is some degree of cognitive learning, where people explore different thoughts about themselves and the outside world. Some therapies are quite explicit about this, and spend a lot of time working on constructs and ideas. Probably the vast majority of clients, no matter what kind of therapy they are in, spend some of the time thinking about themselves, the ideas and opinions they hold, and the way they make sense out of their experiences.

All of these things take place, in varying degrees, in all forms of therapy. They can be thought of as the background to the therapy in that they may not be what is specifically being sought after, but are present nonetheless. Specific techniques, methods and therapeutic interventions are designed to promote specific kinds of experiences. If, for example, a therapy has cathartic release of pent-up emotion as a major goal, its techniques will reflect this. Similarly, if a therapy has the development of decision-making strategies as a goal, then its techniques and methods will be skewed in this direction. The factors we have identified as "common elements" will still be present, however, whether they are recognised or not.

What makes Person-Centred therapy different?

Person-Centred therapy, and indeed the whole of the Person-Centred Approach, rests on the premise that within each of us are to be found the resources and personal power needed to effect positive personality change. These resources can become mobilised more easily within relationships in which we feel understood, respected and valued. So much is clear from everything we have written so far in this book.

Everything the therapist or the facilitator does needs to be consistent with this philosophy if therapy is to be effective. We cannot, as has already been pointed out, compromise on these fundamental principles - trusting our clients to discover what is best for them one moment, and directing them towards some goal of our own the next.

Diagnosis

Person-Centred therapy is not interested in providing labels to describe aspects of human experience wherever these labels tend to objectify or generalise that experience. You will not find anywhere in Carl Rogers' writings any list of diagnostic labels like "neurotic", "obsessional", "compulsive" etc., or any advice on how to recognise such "conditions" or a suggested therapeutic "treatment".

Staying in the client's frame of reference

It is fundamental to the practice of Person-Centred therapy that the therapist tries at all times to enter into the client's world, and stay there. The therapist is concerned with understanding how life is experienced by individual clients, how they defend themselves against allowing experiences into awareness, and how they distort or deny their experiences each in their own idiosyncratic ways. The therapist is also concerned with the client's feelings of self-esteem (or the lack of it), the client's frustrated need for self-regard, and the clients unique conditions of worth.

Suggestion, interpretation and treatment

Since the therapist trusts completely in the client's capacity to change, and in the existence of the actualising tendency, he or she is concerned to support and nurture the client's personal power, self understanding and exercise of choice. To suggest ways in which the client might change, or to lead the client along preselected pathways would be an abandonment of the principle that it is the client who knows what hurts, and it is only the client who can self-actualise in directions which follow from acknowledgement, acceptance, and learning from that hurt.

Interpretation of a client's feelings, thoughts or behaviour happens against a theoretical system that has some explanation for those experiences. For example, in psychodynamic therapy, interpretation takes place against the background of Freudian drive theory. In Person-Centred theory there is no "explanatory framework" for behaviour other than the fact that the actualising tendency is viewed as the only motivational force.

Offering interpretations of feelings and behaviour is not considered part of Person-Centred therapy because an interpretation must originate from within the therapist's frame of reference, not the client's. We are not trying to suggest that the process of interpretation is wrong or misguided in other contexts, only that it is inconsistent with Person-Centred principles. Interpretation plays an important role in psychodynamic therapy and is consistent with that therapeutic philosophy.

To provide treatment, in the classic sense of diagnosing a condition and deciding on an appropriate treatment plan, would run counter to the principle that the resources for change lie within the client, not within the therapist or his techniques.

Human beings are constructive and social

People become destructive, evil or anti-social because they are attempting to protect themselves from further hurt, and are engaged in actualising a damaged and conditional self. This is not the same as saying that human beings are good, which is a common mistake that people attribute wrongly to Carl Rogers. The basic direction of the actualising tendency is towards a constructive self in which the development and expression of potential is its major purpose.

Relationships are the key to growth

Human beings live in social groups and affect and influence each other. According to Person-Centred theory, people become who they are largely as a result of the characteristics and qualities of the relationships they have experienced between themselves and others. Relationships, particularly very early ones, affect each person's developing sense of self, and provide experiences which may either nurture or damage the emerging self. Person-Centred therapists try to provide clients with relationships in which negative conditions of worth can become exposed, re-evaluated and, where necessary, dispensed with. In other words, the therapist tries to provide a relationship with the positive, nurturing qualities that were, perhaps, unavailable in the client's early relationships when they were most needed.

The gradual building of a therapeutic relationship based on the three core conditions discussed earlier is not a preparation for any other activity, nor is it simply a process of establishing rapport. *There is no other approach to psychotherapy that operates from this principle,* and therefore it becomes very difficult, if not impossible, to see how Person-Centred therapy can be combined with any other approach. Techniques and methods imported from other approaches, which almost always take the form of direct interventions, would be inconsistent with Person-Centred philosophy.

Flexibility and creativity within Person-Centred therapy

There is always room within the Person-Centred Approach for therapists to develop their creativity and originality *and maintain philosophical and theoretical consistency*. We'd like to give a brief example of this from the experience of one of us *(TM)*.

The client was a young woman clothes designer with a lot of creative and artistic talent, who I shall call Sally. She came into therapy because she felt, in her words, "fragmented", that she didn't have a "sense of being a solid person", and that she was always "all over the place, hardly ever finishing anything, always forgetting where I'm supposed to be."

We had five sessions together, and things seemed to be going well enough. She was talking and expressing quite a lot of feeling, and I felt my empathy to be quite strong with her. Suddenly, in the sixth session this exchange happened:

Sally: *All this talking and I feel there is still some part of me missing in all this. I'm not really a talker, I get stuck with what I'm trying to say. It's not so much like that when I paint or draw, then I can really get into something for hours on end. I don't get the same sense of frustration.*

TM: *I thought I'd been picking up that frustration for a while now. It seems like you do have things you want to say, but they don't come out somehow, that you have other ways of saying things, and they feel better for you.*

Sally: *If I could paint you a picture now, I think it might say something about me, I don't know what though.*

TM: *Are you saying you'd like to try it and see what happens?*

Sally really did want to try this. I had come close to making a suggestion, or offering some kind of direction, but I was thinking that this had come from Sally, not me. She had initiated the idea of drawing or painting something, and I didn't know what she would do, and I had no idea how we might use it after she had done it.

I gave Sally some A5 sheets of white paper, and my collection of felt tipped pens, pencils and crayons that my children use, and sat back while she settled down to her art work. After about twenty minutes she had finished, and she handed the sheet of paper over to me.

Sally: *What do you see?*

TM: *You have drawn a woman, who looks quite old to me, older than you anyway. She is looking into the distance, shading her eyes from the sun. She is wearing what I know as a Harlequin outfit, made up of black and white diamonds. The only colour in the picture is her bright yellow hair.*

Sally: *Well of course, it's me. I can't see where I'm going because the light is in my eyes. The suit is all the bits of me, black and white. First a black bit, then a white bit, then another black bit. This bit of me is like this, then the next bit is the opposite. That's how I am, first one thing, then the other.*

TM: *And that's how it feels to be you, I guess. You can't see where you're going to end up, or where you're headed, and first you think you're this, then the next minute, something else....*

Sally: *Yes, but look, I've just realised this...the suit is made up of patches stitched together, the design isn't just printed on...but when you look at it all together, it does add up to something definite. It's like all the bits do add up to me, if you like.*

TM: *So it's possible then, that the bits are not so separate, they have all been stitched together to make something whole.....*

Sally: *Do you mean that the suit can be made up of opposite bits, but still add up to something if you put them in the right order?*

TM: *Well, you said it first!*

This is an example of how working in a way completely consistent with Person-Centred theory enabled the dialogue to shift for a time into a different mode of expression. Another example is of a client who completely re-arranged the furniture in the room to symbolise the different ways he felt about himself, and the different relationships he had with people. Again, this was something he thought of himself, and it really worked well for this client for whom words did not come easily. It is fair to say, though, that in our experience this sort of thing does not happen often. Person-Centred therapy does tend to rely a lot on words.

Right at the beginning of this book we said that we did not want to persuade you that Person-Centred ideas were necessarily any better than the ideas contained within many other approaches to therapy. Our aim was to share our understandings and experiences with you, so that you can decide for yourself how far you feel comfortable with the ideas as we described them. If we have managed to give you some information, and make Person-Centred therapy come alive, even a little bit, then we have succeeded in our original aim.

The next checklist will help you think about how far you see yourself as Person-Centred. How much you agree with the statements contained in it will help you to decide if your heart (and head) lies with the Person-Centred Approach, or elsewhere.

CHECKLIST 8: HOW PERSON-CENTRED ARE YOU?

1. Deep down, each person is social, positive and trying to become more of who they are.

2. Within each of us lies the capacity and resources to change and grow towards becoming fully functioning.

3. The goal of therapy is the self-actualisation and full congruence of the client.

4. The goal of the therapist is to create a relationship of mutual trust and safety in which clients can discover more and more of themselves.

5. The therapist's way of working relies on values and attitudes, not techniques.

6. The therapist values encountering clients on a person-to-person level.

7. Clients grow and develop in therapy without therapists evaluating, judging or directing them.

8. In Person-Centred therapy, it is the relationship of specific qualities existing between therapist and client that matters.

9. The content and direction of therapy is a matter to be decided by clients, not therapists.

10. Diagnosis, developing treatment plans, and setting goals and targets are not useful activities for the Person-Centred therapist.

We must now bring the main part of this book to a close. The next chapter gives some suggestions for further reading, and gives some advice about choosing a training course in Person-Centred therapy.

We hope you have enjoyed reading this book as much as we enjoyed writing it. We have written positively and optimistically about therapy, about the infinite possibilities for personal growth and change, and about how we feel we have grown and developed through our contact with Carl Rogers and the Person-Centred Approach.

Although we are optimistic, we are also realistic. We think therapy, almost any kind of therapy, can do a lot, but we also know it can't do everything. Sometimes human problems are just so complex, so mystifying and so profound that nothing seems to help. We mustn't start making exaggerated claims for therapy, just because we feel we have benefitted from it so much ourselves.

This final checklist finishes on an optimistic note.

CHECKLIST 9: WHAT THERAPY CAN'T AND CAN DO
Therapy can't:

1. Change the past.

2. Guarantee a positive future.

3. Change the world.

4. Help everybody.

5. Change your economic or social circumstances.

6. Guarantee happiness.

7. Solve insoluble problems.

Therapy can:

1. Help you understand yourself better.

2. Help you talk through your problems.

3. Allow present feelings to emerge and be expressed.

4. Allow past feelings to be re-experienced and re-evaluated.

5. Allow present life situations to be explored and considered.

6. Enable more informed decision making.

7. Help you get more out of life.

8. Help you put more into life.

9. Help you enjoy better relationships.

10. Help you become more of who you are.

CHAPTER NINE

RESOURCES

1. Books

There are now so many books about all kinds of counselling and psychotherapy (and this is one more), that it can be difficult to choose the most useful. It isn't usually very helpful to be confronted with a list of thirty or more books, all with interesting sounding titles, especially when you are just starting out to explore the literature available.

We give here some titles of the books we have found most helpful over the last few years. Rather than just give the title and author, we have added a few words of commentary which we hope will help you decide where to start.

In our opinion, the best place to start is with *On Becoming a Person* (Constable, 1961). This is Rogers' best known book, and it includes a complete description of the Person-Centred Approach as it applies to counselling and psychotherapy.

Also excellent is *A Way of Being*, (Houghton Mifflin 1980). This is many people's favourite because it is written in a very personal and engaging style. In early chapters, Carl Rogers describes some of the influences on his own life, and looks back over his long career a therapist researche an teacher Othe goo chapter ar 'Empathic: An Unappreciated Way of Being', and 'Ellen West - and Loneliness'.

A book that collects together some of Rogers' best writing and most influential papers is called *The Carl Rogers Reader,* edited by H. Kirschenbaum and V. Henderson (Houghton Mifflin, 1989). This is a very valuable source book for anyone interested in the PCA, and it includes chapters on theory and research, education, group work and philosophy as well as on therapy.

A very good introduction to Person-Centred Counselling is *Person-Centred Counselling in Action*, by D. Mearns and B. Thorne (Sage 1988). This is one of the few books on Person-Centred counselling and therapy written by British authors. It covers the theory and practice of counselling in a straightforward, easy to read way, and is very popular with counselling students.

An excellent book that deals with counselling in general is the *Handbook of Counselling in Britain*, edited by W. Dryden, D. Charles-Edwards and R. Woolfe (Routledge, 1989). Although this book is not very flattering about the Person-Centred Approach, it offers lots of useful discussions about different aspects of counselling. Also edited by Dryden is *Individual Therapy - A Handbook* (Open University, 1990). In this book, Person-Centred therapy is clearly and concisely described by Brian Thorne.

For those interested in Person-Centred personality theory, two books are particularly recommended. They are *Personality Theories*, by L. Hjelle and D. Ziegler (McGraw Hill, second edition, 1981), and *Personality* by L. Pervin (John Wiley and Son, fifth edition, 1989). Both of these books deal very well with Rogers' personality theory, and show how it is applied in therapy and other human relationships.

A new biography of Carl Rogers has recently been published, *Carl Rogers*, by B. Thorne (Sage 1992). This will give you a very good idea of how Rogers' life and work are so bound up with each other, how Rogers developed his ideas, and how he became so influential in the world of counselling and therapy.

A fairly well known book is *Dibs - In Search of Self,* by V. Axline (Victor Gollancz, 1966). This is a book about "play therapy", and recounts the struggle of a hurt small boy to come to terms with his life and find a new direction for himself. Virginia Axline was a student of Carl Rogers, and the book is written with a Person-Centred point of view.

CHAPTER NINE

A book that is generally useful for counsellors and others in the helping professions is *Counselling and Psychology for Health Professionals,* edited by R. Bayne and P. Nicolson (Chapman Hall, 1993). Particularly useful are the chapters on supervision, by Ian Horton, and the social context of counselling by Jenny Bimrose.

One of the most popular introductory books to counselling psychology is *Three Psychologies*, by R. Nye (Brooks/Cole, 1975). This book compares the theories of Freud, Skinner and Rogers, and explains how their theories are applied in counselling and psychotherapy. It is very readable and concise.

Although not directly connected with the Person-Centred Approach, many Person-Centred counsellors find the books by Alice Miller very useful and stimulating as she seems to have much sympathy with Rogers' views, though she never makes reference to Rogers directly. Try *Thou Shalt Not be Aware* (Virago, 1985) and *The Drama of Being a Child* (Virago, 1987).

Another book in this What is...? series, *What is Counselling?* by P. Burnard (Gale Centre, 1992) discusses some of Rogers' work, as well as providing a useful, general introduction to a number of approaches to counselling. We hope, though, that we have gone some way towards correcting the impression given by Burnard that Person-Centred therapy over-emphasises individualism (we think it is about living better with ourselves and others), and that Rogers thought that people are basically "good", (a common misunderstanding of what Rogers actually said). Unfortunately, Burnard goes on to say that "client-centred therapy is based on a fundamental belief in the 'natural goodness' of persons". In fact, it is based on the theory of actualisation, which is nothing to do with 'natural goodness' at all. We are also a bit puzzled by Burnard's reference to "evangelists" in what he calls "the client-centred movement", particularly as Rogers was concerned that Person-Centred therapy should not be associated in people's minds with himself as a personality, and objected very strongly to the term 'Rogerian' whenever he got the chance. Of course Person-Centred therapists believe that their approach to therapy is an effective one, but we have never met one who believes that Person-Centred therapy is "the answer to everything", which is what Burnard claims of some, though he doesn't give any evidence to support this claim.

What is Psychotherapy? by D. Gale (Gale Centre, 1989) has some interesting and thought provoking ideas about therapy generally, but Derek Gale hardly mentions Carl Rogers at all, though this is not all that unusual in books and articles about therapy and counselling. Many of them describe the core conditions, and discuss the importance of the therapeutic relationship in ways that are very similar to basic Person-Centred ideas, but for some reason fail to acknowledge the source of the ideas and concepts they deal with. On one level, this does not matter at all as it is the ideas that count more than who happened to originate them. On the other hand it does seem to us that Rogers deserves some credit and acknowledgement for the important contributions he made to our understanding of the process of therapy.

2. Training in Person-Centred therapy and counselling

Training to become a counsellor or therapist can be a lengthy and expensive process, and there are very few courses in Further and Higher Education institutes that are exclusively Person-Centred. Most provide a general training in a number of approaches, or compare and contrast one approach with another. A brand new course, which is totally Person-Centred is at Jordanhill College, Glasgow. This course is available by both full and part-time study, and it is possible also to read for an MPhil degree in counselling psychology at Jordanhill. (Write to David Mearns, Coordinator, Strathclyde University Counselling Unit, University of Strathclyde, Glasgow, G13 1PP).

Courses in counselling are also available at, for example, the University of East London, the University of Hertfordshire, Manchester University, Leicester University, University College of Ripon and York St. John, City University and Liverpool University. These courses are not strictly Person-Centred, though many are more or less heavily influenced by Person-Centred ideas. An exception is the course at Leicester University, which has a psychodynamic orientation. Many colleges run counselling courses that last from a few months to two or three years, but it is not possible here to give a comprehensive list of all the counselling courses available. For more information, write to the British Association for Counselling, 1, Regents Place, Rugby, Warwickshire, for a copy of the Directory of Training in Counselling and Psychotherapy (ninth edition, £8 to non-members).

If you do a course at a public Institute of Further or Higher Education, you can be assured that the course being offered is subject to a strict quality control procedure, and that the qualification you receive will have some credibility. In the private sector, things are not so clear cut, but with the advent of the BAC Courses Recognition Scheme you can now apply to a BAC Recognised Course in the knowledge that it has gone through a rigorous screening.

Completing a BAC Recognised Course means that when you come to apply to BAC for professional accreditation as a counsellor, BAC will assume that their training criteria for accreditation have been met. You will still, however, have to satisfy the BAC criteria of experience of counselling clients under supervision, before you can be accredited. (Some courses at public institutions are also BAC Recognised, for example the Post-Graduate Diploma in Counselling at the University of East London, and the Counselling Diploma at the University of Hertfordshire).

There are now a number of BAC Recognised courses which are either completely, or substantially Person-Centred. Examples are the courses at the Metanoia Institute in London (13, North Common Road, Ealing, London W5), Person-Centred Therapy (Britain), (c/o Brian Thorne, The Norwich Centre, 7, Earlham Road, Norwich), and the course run by the Institute for Person-Centred Learning (220, Ashurst Drive, Barkingside, Ilford, Essex) which has recently successfully completed the Recognition process.

In order for a course to gain BAC Recognition it must be of a substantial duration (more than 400 contact hours). It must also be able to offer appropriate theory and skills training and have a coherent core model or approach to counselling. In addition, it must, for example, make adequate arrangements for the supervision of trainees in their client work, and have a suitably qualified and experienced staff team who adhere to the BAC Code of Ethics for trainers.

If a course does not have BAC Recognition, this does not, by any means, indicate that it is not a good course. The Recognition process is still quite new, and some courses are still coming to terms with the fairly tough criteria established by BAC. There are many good courses that have fewer than 400 contact hours, and there are courses which do not wish to enter the Recognition process for one reason or another.

The best advice, if you are thinking of going in for a training course in the private sector, is to talk to some of the existing students and the staff about what they do and how they do it. Ask around to see whether the course has a good reputation, and whether the staff are well enough qualified and experienced in training. Take the cost into account when making your decision, but remember that many training courses do a lot of their work in residential settings, and this is bound to be expensive. If the course is BAC Recognised you can have confidence that it will be properly run by experienced staff, and if it isn't properly organised you can complain to the BAC and get things put right.

Finally, if you would like to take your interest in the Person-Centred Approach further, you can now join the British Association for the Person-Centred Approach (BM BAPCA, London, WC1N 3XX). You will receive regular newsletters and the twice-yearly journal *Person-Centred Practice* which will put you in touch with other Person-Centred practitioners in the UK. We wish you well and hope to meet you at a Person-Centred workshop or seminar some day.

ADDRESS LIST

Associations

The British Association for the Person-Centred Approach
BM BAPCA
London WC1N 3XX

Association for the Development of the Person-Centred Approach,
Box 6881
San Carlos,
CA 94070-6881,
USA

The British Association for Counselling,
1, Regents Place,
Rugby,
Warwickshire,
CV21 2PJ

The Association for Humanistic Psychology
Box 3582
London WC1N 3XX

The Facilitator Development Institute,
c/o Mhairi Macmillan,
Student Counselling Centre,
University of St. Andrews,
College Gate,
St. Andrews,
Fyfe,
Scotland, KY16 6AJ

The Person-Centred Approach Network,
109, Rupert Street,
Norwich,
NR2 2AU

The Association for Person-Centred Therapy in Scotland,
40, Kelvingrove St,
Glasgow,
G3 7RZ

Person-Centred Art Therapy Centre,
c/o Liesl Silverstone,
17, Cranbourne Gardens,
London,
NW11 0HN

Journals

Person-Centred Practice
255, Coventry Road,
Ilford,
Essex,
IG1 4RF

The Person-Centred Journal,
Aderhold 402,
University of Georgia,
Athens,
Ga. 30602,
USA

Self and Society
18, Lower Street,
Stroud,
Gloucestershire,
GL5 2HT

Counselling (Journal of the BAC)
1, Regents Place,
Rugby,
Warwickshire,
CV21 2PJ

The Journal of Humanistic Pyschology, (Subscriptions)
Sage Publications,
6, Bonhill Street,
London,
EC2A 4PU

SELECTED INDEX

Page numbers indicate where the definition or description of the key words in the text are to be found.

THE 'WHAT IS' SERIES

This series of books on counselling is unique, because each author starts from a personal perspective, hence the subtitle 'A Personal and Practical Guide'. The theoretical explanations are presented along with the writers' personal experience of counselling and therapy, so at the same time as learning about the field covered by each volume, the reader discovers something about the author and how he came to be a practitioner in that particular field. Each book is a self study guide with exercises, check lists and activities which can be used for individual and group study.

Each title includes a clear description of the type of therapy, examples of how it is used, reading lists and information on training. This series is specially useful to counselling courses as the self study format is ideally suited for supplementing the course teaching.

The Series Editor is Derek Gale who is well known for his regular column in *Counselling* and for his controversial and exciting views on the subject of counselling and psychotherapy.

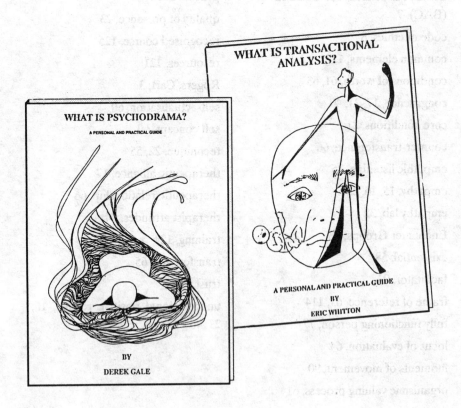